PROFESSIONAL PRESENCE

ALSO BY SUSAN BIXLER

The Professional Image

PROFESSIONAL PRESENCE

◆

THE TOTAL PROGRAM FOR GAINING THAT EXTRA EDGE IN BUSINESS—BY AMERICA'S TOP CORPORATE IMAGE CONSULTANT

Susan Bixler

PHOTOS BY THE PROFESSIONAL IMAGE, INC.

A Perigee Book

To my courageous husband, Jose,
and to our son, Christopher,
who is the light of our lives.

Perigee Books
are published by
The Putnam Publishing Group
200 Madison Avenue
New York, NY 10016

First Perigee Edition 1992

Library of Congress Cataloging-in-Publication Data

Bixler, Susan.
Professional presence : the total program for gaining that extra
edge in business—by America's top corporate image consultant /
Susan Bixler ; photos by the Professional Image, Inc.—1st Perigee ed.
p.   cm.
Originally published: New York : G.P. Putnam's Sons © 1991. With new introd.
Includes index.
ISBN 0-399-51786-3 (acid-free paper)
1. Business etiquette.   2. Office politics.   I. Title.
[HF5389.B57   1992   92-9751   CIP
650.1′3—dc20

Cover photo © 1991 by Bernard Cohen
Hairstyling on models by P. J. Nicholson
Photograph of the author © 1991 by Debi Greene-Davenport,
assisted by Mylinda Coleman

Printed in the United States of America

1   2   3   4   5   6   7   8   9   10

This book is printed on acid-free paper.
∞

With Gratitude and Grateful Acknowledgment

Judy Linden: My editor, who put tremendous energy and her own unique talent into this book. Judy embodies to perfection every aspect of professional presence herself.

Lynn Seligman: My agent, who over the period of three long years never wavered in her support and enthusiasm of this project. Lynn is in a rarefied class of professionals.

Sheri Underwood: My company associate, who is my most loyal fan and treasured confidante.

And to all my clients and friends who read the manuscript and contributed generously of their time, experience, and knowledge of business: Ruth Ackerman; Janis Allen; Joanne Bixler-Clifton; Stephen Dana; David Deans; Randi Marie Freidig; Lynne Henderson; Beverly Langford; Dewitt Mitchell; Cori Nickerson; Beth Nilsson; Margarita Porto; Russ Umphenour; Sandra Brouwer-Wright; and Thomas Lee Wright.

Part I

◆

WHAT IS PROFESSIONAL PRESENCE?

CONTENTS

CONTENTS

INTRODUCTION

The mystique of power, presence, and control has long fascinated business professionals. It is an intangible quality that can produce extremely tangible results. In business, we want others immediately to recognize our presence as being self-assured and thoroughly competent. We want to be able to impart a confidence that others can quickly discern and actually experience the first time they meet us.

How do we do it? Can "presence" be broken down into component parts? Can "presence" even be broken down at all?

I'll answer my own rhetorical question: Certainly it can. That is what Professional Presence is all about. It is a look at the intricate puzzle pieces of power, control, and self-assurance.

As president and founder of the largest corporate image consulting firm, The Professional Image, Inc., I have been totally immersed in the image consulting business since 1979. This has afforded me a broad perspective of the "growing up of image and presence in America." I also have an organization of over two hundred professional image consultants, who have gone through my training programs and who have provided me with their perspective on image in corporate America.

After more than a decade of presenting scores of image seminars to over one thousand of America's finest and most admired companies, what continues to inspire me are the "light bulbs" that light up during my presentation. Opportunities, events, and situations that may have been previously ignored or poorly handled, will, after a seminar on presence, be met with skill and confidence.

Professional Presence is a coming together of twelve years of information presented at my seminars. Of course, my own business experiences and observations outside of the seminar environment comprise part of the data in this book. Since the inception of my company, I have also met with business people, both on an individual and group basis, to discuss presence and how it is interpreted in their industry. This book is a synthesis of all three perspectives.

Gaining professional presence doesn't mean that embarrassing or difficult situations disappear. For example, I met with an executive from one of the large telephone systems who greeted me with a firm handshake, a confident smile, and a gracious manner. We discussed my program, set a date for the seminar, and then stood up to shake hands.

An argyle sock that had clung to her slip, through the marvel of static electricity, decided to disengage itself at that exact moment. As the sock dropped on the carpet next to her shoe, we both stared at it and gasped. Embarrassed, but laughing, she swooped down to pick it up and said, "So this is where all my misplaced socks hang out. No wonder I can never find them!"

She acknowledged the situation, recovered quickly using humor, and generally handled the entire situation in a way that gave her additional presence. From my observation, she ranks at the top of the list of those who possess a powerful presence. It's not what happens to us, it is how we handle it that will set up apart.

Professional presence has more to do with negotiation than with manipulation. It rarely intimidates, at least not intentionally. Having presence is not being destructively powerful. It is not being "superior" or creating an "inferior." It is bringing everyone up to the same level of confidence.

Professional presence is a blend of poise, self-confidence, control, style, and savoir-faire that can empower us to command respect in any situation.

Professional presence is approaching every business situation with a strong belief in our skills and a clear knowledge of how our presence will impress and impact others.

The business world requires from us a range of behavior. We deal with people of varying backgrounds and experiences, and it becomes imperative that we adapt to constantly changing, often sensitive situations. Simply understanding numbers doesn't make a great CPA, banker, salesperson, or stockbroker. But our ability to handle ourselves well does contribute to the making of a great CPA, banker, salesperson, stockbroker, or any other professional in business.

Making an impressive entrance, self-promoting, managing a meeting, mastering office politics, knowing what to say and to whom, handling a romance in the office, defusing embarrassment, understanding contemporary manners, dining, dealing and finessing your way through a corporate event are the pieces that make up the powerful mosaic of presence.

Professional Presence strikes a much-needed balance between business etiquette and the "power" philosophies of the early eighties. It shows that the two approaches can actually come together and enhance each other. This book is for the nineties—a mature recognition that strength and diplomacy have always gone hand in hand.

Ultimately, professional presence is understanding how each of us can use the power of our own presence to feel fulfilled, empowered, and successful. Professional presence produces results: It helps give us focus, momentum, and control over our business environment.

Learning to create presence is one of the most valuable skills we can ever acquire in business. It is increasingly important in this fast-paced and competitive world.

I spoke to a group of librarians at their annual meeting in Florida. They listened, nodded slightly, and applauded politely at the end of my presentation, in much the same manner that the groups who follow golf pros around the course do. I felt sick afterwards. I knew I had "bombed." I stood off to the side and waited with apprehension next to the table that had copies of my book.

The man who had hired me to present the program came up, shook my hand, and said, "I have never seen this group so enthusiastic. Did you hear that applause!" I stared at him in disbelief. I thought he was being sarcastic. But as I searched his face for traces of irony, there were none. He was sincere. They had liked and learned from my presentation.

My objective with Professional Presence is the same one that I have for every one of my seminars: I want to offer you new and valuable insights and information. I also want to confirm the many things that you are doing right, because with affirmation they can become an even stronger part of your total presence.

It is a pleasure and a privilege for me to offer you my advice, observations, and counsel in addition to the experiences of my esteemed clients and friends—who are usually one in the same. I sincerely believe that this book will give you all the skills necessary to showcase your abilities and that your power and presence will become formidable, recognized, and appreciated in business!

CHAPTER ONE

RECOGNIZING PROFESSIONAL PRESENCE

The important meeting is about to begin. The door swings open and in she walks, striding confidently and decisively into the room, meticulously groomed, immaculately dressed. She greets colleagues with a firm handshake, looking them squarely in the eye, calling those she knows by name and introducing herself to those she doesn't.

Or, you see him in a critical situation. His very position in the chair denotes his self-assurance. If things get tense he deals with the conflict fairly and productively; angry outbursts don't seem to rattle him. He understands the value of good manners; he's in control and those around him know it.

A BREED APART

The special quality that sets certain business people apart, that creates power, credibility, and a sense of competence is professional presence. A potent and dynamic blend of poise, self-confidence, control, style, and savoir-faire, it empowers us to be able to command respect in any situation. It is *not* a heavy-handed manipulation of others. It rarely intimidates—at least not intentionally.

Across corporate America, one of the issues that we are all facing is that our credentials are often not much different from those of other professionals. How can we stand out in a job interview, a sales call, or an important meeting? Acquiring professional presence will help us pull away from the crowd. It affords us distinction and power.

ADAPT OR BECOME EXTINCT

Today's business environment demands more than keeping our nose to the grindstone and our in-basket empty. Because we conduct business in an arena with people of varying backgrounds and experiences, we must learn how to deal with and adapt to constantly changing, often sensitive situations.

Professional presence is the savvy that gives us as business people the edge, an extra measure of control. It enables us to act in any situation with clear advantage, without making other people feel uncomfortable.

Professional presence means commanding attention every time we walk into a room. It also means running a meeting with a strong style, being comfortable at a business retreat, self-promoting effectively, handling gossip, understanding romance, telling jokes, breaking bread, entertaining clients, and knowing when to leave your spouse at home. It is comprised of all the resources that we have to influence others.

Professional presence is a mature recognition that strength and diplomacy have always gone hand in hand and that far more can be negotiated than forced. Professional presence is a subtle but powerful form of negotiating for the best circumstance, vantage point, and opportunity.

The way we present ourselves in business affects our promotability, our effectiveness with associates, and how customers perceive us. It is the best way to showcase our educational credentials and our experience.

WHAT IS YOUR PPQ? (PROFESSIONAL PRESENCE QUOTIENT)

One of the ways I like to measure the knowledge that my seminar attendees have gained during one of my sessions is to test them by using true or false questions before and after the seminar. They are usually amazed at how many image and presence questions they simply cannot answer.

By testing your base of information before you read this book, you will have concrete proof by the end of the book of how much you have learned from Professional Presence. After taking the PPQ, check your responses against the answers at the end of the test.

PROFESSIONAL PRESENCE QUOTIENT

X T (F)   1. A limp handshake can, at times, create a more powerful impression than a strong clasp.

(T) F   2. Changing a meeting location can often change the attitude of a meeting.

T (F)   3. Don't waste your time on "waiting room" literature, like company newsletters, in a reception area.

T (F)   4. A man should wait for a woman in business to offer her hand.

(T) F   5. The person with the highest rank in business is always mentioned first in an introduction. Gender is not a consideration.

(T) F   6. In an office setting, select the arm chair, not the sofa.

X T (F)   7. Exchange business cards at the beginning of the meeting.

X T (F)   8. Every industry has its own wardrobe requirements. One standard cannot fit everyone.

X T (F)   9. Skirt lengths should be determined by the leg shape and the industry.

(T) F 10. Men generally get their suit interest from a pattern, not from color or unusual styling.

(T) F 11. Women generally get their suit interest from color or unusual styling, not pattern.

(T) F 12. More expensive wool is generally softer and causes less itching and allergic reaction.

T (F) 13. Braces (suspenders) and belts are worn together.

(T) F 14. Eyeglasses can make a business person look richer and smarter.

(T) F 15. Long, acrylic nails are a dated look.

(T) F 16. Beautiful teeth project an image of good breeding and good health.

(T) F 17. A decisive statement can be negated by weak body language.

(T) F 18. It is easier to influence others and exert status in person than over the phone or by letter.

T (F) 19. The best way to handle a chit-chatter is to look anxiously at your watch.

✗ T (F) 20. Heaving your shoulders and shooting a cryptic look is a stronger message than your verbal one.

(T) F 21. If someone repeats a sentence several times while looking at the floor, swallowing hard, and putting a hand in front of the mouth, they are probably lying.

(T) F 22. The use of silence is a powerful way to establish presence.

T (F) 23. Taking notes at a meeting is rather rude because you must break eye contact to do it.

(T) F 24. The most effective meetings are no more than 30 minutes.

T (F) 25. Don't provide an agenda unless it is a large meeting.

✗ (T) F 26. Recapping information for latecomers is a considerate thing to do.

(T) F 27. At a meeting, make eye contact with each person until you have determined the color of their eyes.

T (F) 28. If you want consensus, don't try to break up seating arrangements at a hostile meeting because people like to define their comfort zone.

T F 29. The power perch is the seat to the right of the head of the table.

T F 30. Sit as close to the leader as protocol permits.

T F 31. The office grapevine is 50% accurate.

T F 32. Less than 1% of the population can keep a secret.

T F 33. Keeping up with a client's sports interest is a form of courtesy.

T F 34. It is generally inappropriate to ask an established customer what their weekend plans entail.

T F 35. Business people who are current on news events are generally considered current on business issues, too.

T F 36. If the moment presents itself, name-drop.

T F 37. It is impossible to be considered sophisticated without a working knowledge of manners.

T F 38. If a joke is not funny, but not offensive, laugh anyway.

T F 39. The only time to privately call attention to someone's appearance or behavior mistake is when they can do something about it.

T F 40. Creating a calm presence is particularly important when you have made a severe faux pas.

T F 41. Reacting to someone's embarrassment by trying to share in the blame is a gracious gesture.

T F 42. Don't associate yourself with negative employees, because you will become viewed as negative by association.

T F 43. If you are having an affair at the office, never tell your boss.

X T (F) 44. Romantic chemistry is part of every large business environment.

T (F) 45. Finding someone else to date within the office helps get over an office affair.

(T) F 46. Don't become the sounding board for an "involved" associate.

(T) F 47. Before you begin an office affair, look at the consequences of how it could end.

X (T) F 48. Voice mail is a very mechanical method of transmitting information and will cause you to lose presence.

X T (F) 49. Sending a facsimile can create more urgency than a letter.

X T F 50. Cartoon transmittal sheets lighten up any message and are especially good for negative information.

X (T) F 51. A well-written, well-intended thank-you letter can be faxed.

(T) -F 52. Standing up while on the phone will enhance the quality of your voice.

(T) F 53. Get on someone's appointment calendar with an important phone call the same way you would an in-person appointment.

X (T) F 54. Return all phone calls within 48 hours.

T (F) 55. If you have a choice, refrain from traveling with your boss.

(T) F 56. Luggage is just as important as a briefcase in terms of appearance.

(T) F 57. A dirty car has been proven to create a depressed driver.

X T (F) 58. It is appropriate to wear casual clothing on a business flight.

(T) F   59. Trying a new restaurant with a client can prove to be disastrous.

T (F)   60. At a business lunch, because time is limited, begin business discussions as soon as you sit down.

(T) F   61. Hard liquor should be reserved for dinner meetings only.

(T) F   62. Dinner is the best choice for a business meal because it is leisurely, elegant, and relationship building.

(T) F   63. Don't take medicines in front of business clients.

(T) F   64. As the host of a meal you, not your guests, should request additional water, coffee, or special service.

T (F)   65. It is correct to let a client eat an appetizer alone.

(T) F   66. If the bill is wrong, quietly point it out to the waitperson when they pass your table.

(T) F   67. Tipping the attendant for your customer's car is good manners and good business.

(T) F   68. It is garish to eat the garnish on your plate.

(T) F   69. A limousine for a business event is sometimes an excellent investment when crowds and parking present a problem.

T (F)   70. The empty seat at most corporate meetings is usually next to the CEO or president.

(T) F   71. Most people's comfort zone is with their peers.

T (F)   72. Wearing a dark suit to a black-tie corporate affair is considered acceptable in today's business.

(T) F   73. "Business casual" attire has the emphasis more on business than on casual.

T (F)   74. A little gossip about your boss will help loosen up the conversation with co-workers.

(T) F   75. Eating before a business event is considered smart if you have a large appetite.

T F 76. Don't order anything that can't be eaten attractively, like corn on the cob, juicy hamburgers, and pasta with tomato sauce.

T F 77. When considering sports with a client, be honest about your playing ability.

T F 78. Don't miss your boss's big speech at the company meeting.

T F 79. Generally decline a pool party invitation if you are female.

T F 80. It is considered bad form to invite a good customer to an in-house company office party.

T F 81. If your spouse is clearly not a business asset, include him or her in only the largest and most anonymous of corporate events.

T F 82. If you are single, always bring a date to a business affair.

T F 83. Always bring an invited spouse or companion up to date on pertinent business information prior to a business event.

T F 84. The corporate spouse of a highly placed executive is generally welcome at most dinner meetings.

T F 85. The trend today is to include spouses in as many company-sponsored events as possible.

T F 86. A good corporate gift is a hardcover book, a brass clock, a video of a favorite old movie, or a bottle of wine.

T F 87. If a corporate gift has a logo on it, it doesn't have to be of good quality. Inexpensive gifts with a nice note are very acceptable.

T F 88. Service gifts like tickets for an exclusive sporting event, concert, theater performance, or round of golf at a country club don't have the same impact as a tangible gift.

T (F) 89. A gift should be sent for every business invitation that is received.

(T) F 90. Community involvement is part of having professional presence.

ANSWERS

1. True	19. False	37. True	55. False	73. True
2. True	20. True	38. True	56. True	74. False
3. False	21. True	39. True	57. True	75. True
4. False	22. True	40. True	58. False	76. True
5. True	23. False	41. True	59. True	77. True
6. True	24. True	42. True	60. False	78. True
7. True	25. False	43. False	61. True	79. True
8. True	26. False	44. True	62. False	80. False
9. True	27. True	45. False	63. True	81. True
10. True	28. False	46. True	64. True	82. False
11. True	29. False	47. True	65. False	83. True
12. True	30. True	48. False	66. False	84. False
13. False	31. False	49. True	67. True	85. False
14. True	32. True	50. False	68. False	86. False
15. True	33. True	51. False	69. True	87. False
16. True	34. False	52. True	70. True	88. False
17. True	35. True	53. True	71. True	89. False
18. True	36. True	54. False	72. False	90. True

If your total score was 85 or above, you have a great deal of professional presence knowledge and will be able to use this book to affirm many of the things you are already doing correctly and fine-tune others.

If your total score was 75 to 84, you know many of the basics, but this book will help fill in the more sophisticated or complex issues inherent in image.

If your total score was less than 74, this book will provide you with all the basics plus an understanding of more advanced skills.

In all cases, after you have read Professional Presence, please go back and retake the PPQ. I can promise an increased awareness and probably a perfect score!

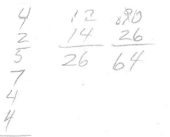

CHAPTER TWO

FIRST IMPRESSIONS, LASTING IMPRESSIONS

At the first company picnic I ever attended, I was determined to make a good first impression. I spotted my boss and made eye contact with the new CEO standing beside him. Suddenly, Nick, a regional manager with a reputation for unwanted kisses, hugs, and jabs, intercepted me, waving his cigar. He shouted, "Hey, Sue, I heard you lost the Melrose account. A six-footer like you should sit down more. Those guys at Melrose are midgets. Ha. Ha."

As an up-and-coming employee of the company, I couldn't ignore Nick. It seemed that everyone was looking at me, waiting to see what I would do.

So I took charge of the encounter. I didn't wait for Nick to grab me, slap me on the back, and further assault me with his typical, "How's your lovelife?" I gave him a token smile, a brief nod, minimal eye contact, and offering a limp handshake I moved on purposefully toward my boss and the CEO.

Do I normally recommend a fake smile and no engaging eye contact followed by a fishlike clasp? No. But I do recommend saving strong, forceful facial expressions and firm, connected handshakes for those who deserve respect.

First impressions can be effective or disastrous, but they are always lasting. Our objective in meeting others is to establish comfort, trust, and rapport and it's not always easy.

Some people intentionally create orchestrated power plays to make others feel intimidated. One buyer from a large department store that I formerly called on refused to make eye contact with anyone in sales. When salespeople would walk through her door, she kept her eyes riveted to whatever information was on her desk at the time. She would verbally greet us and even answer questions, but she never looked up. We felt that we were no more important to her than an annoying fly in her office.

The really savvy salespeople would just sit there and not speak. Although their hearts were pounding because she often controlled 40% of their quota, they refused to talk to the top of her head. Until they felt they were receiving the respect they deserved, they just clammed up and waited.

BUCK AND HIS MOOSEHEADS

Another difficulty is to be acknowledged briefly and then summarily ignored and dismissed. I still vividly remember my first visit with the manager of a large furniture company and his orchestrated intimidation. His secretary showed me in, and there sat Buck, leaning back in his chair, black alligator shoes braced against the front of his desk, phone propped against his shoulder. He nodded in brief greeting, and while I waited for him to finish his conversation, I looked around at the mooseheads and other trophies on the wall and the photographs of Buck at the helm of racing speed boats.

When he finished the call, he stayed seated and reached out to shake hands. For me, it was an awkward stretch.

For ten minutes his phone continued to ring, his shoes stayed on the mahogany desk, and the speed boats continued racing around the office. I was out-manned, out-gunned, and I knew it. I realized that if I stayed much longer, I would lose not only the sale but also my self-esteem. So I suggested, "Buck, let's go down to the company cafeteria for a soda."

Not only was Buck unable to transport his speed boats and dead animals to the cafeteria, he also had to keep his feet on the floor. Away from his home turf and telephone, I was able to reestablish myself and make my presentation. After a bad start and a weak first impression, the only course was to change the location and start over.

Although I didn't sell him anything at that meeting, I followed up for six months, and eventually we introduced an entire image program to his sales force.

After the implementation of my program, Buck and I talked about that first meeting. "You know, Susan," he said, "when you took control of that meeting and moved us out of that damn office of mine, that's when I figured you might know your stuff. I decided then that you were someone I wanted to do business with if you could continue to show that you weren't afraid of me.

"In fact, in my old office, I use to sit in an antique barber chair that kept me towering three feet above everyone else. I intimidated at least eighty percent of the people that walked through my door, but I figured that the other twenty percent were the only people that I wanted to do business with anyway!"

So it is possible to overcome intimidation and a bad beginning. Changing the meeting location is one method. But staying unruffled because you know your image is powerful is critically important.

Overcoming intentional intimidation is just one hurdle to conquer in making a powerful first impression. Where to sit, when to smoke cigarettes, what to do in the reception area, how to make impressive physical contact, when to give out business cards, how to make introductions, synchronizing your body language, and how to appear warm and friendly without flirting are the central issues to making an impact.

First, let's look at some forms of physical contact that can create a confusing message.

A KISS IS JUST A KISS . . . OR IS IT?

When I was a regional manager, one of my fellow managers would "air" kiss every female he was introduced to. A business woman would extend her hand for a handshake and Harold would take it, reach for her shoulder with his other hand, and head straight in for a counterfeit smooch.

To those of us who watched Harold in action, two things became obvious. First, rarely was anyone flattered. Nearly everyone was embarrassed, suspicious, or insulted. Secondly, we saw that women who had met Harold before quickly learned to avoid his kisses. They developed the stiff-elbow, step-back counterattack to elude the unwanted embrace and the phony kiss.

Harold thought that his technique was smooth and that his affectionate approach was the best way to endear himself to new female business acquaintances. He viewed it as his personal trademark. He never realized what was happening, that he was clearly building a barrier between himself and his female customers.

Greeting business acquaintances with a kiss is a mistake. Although it may be expected on Rodeo Drive, it is usually out of place on Wall Street or Main Street.

When you kiss a business associate, you are pretending that you immediately share a close relationship. It fools no one and usually creates discomfort, which is exactly the opposite of what you want to accomplish.

There are several exceptions. If your corporate culture or your industry encourages hugs and friendly embraces, then join in if it is part of your own style. If not, don't be coerced into doing it. The second exception is when you are meeting a longtime business *friend* whom you haven't seen for quite a while. A kiss that doesn't leave lipstick marks (if you leave your mark, quickly and casually rub it off) and a big hug show genuine warmth.

But in all cases, it is the woman who decides if a handshake will turn into a kiss. And if her coworker or customer is male, her aboveboard intention should be perfectly clear.

HEY, LOOK ME OVER

Whenever we walk into a room, our clothing, manners, and mannerisms are on display. Others assess our self-confidence and our ability to present ourselves based on about five seconds of information. Each of us has our own signature of professional presence—an indelible statement that we make the instant we step into a room—that should afford us an opportunity to connect immediately.

That's why I advise the "30-second detail check" for maximum impact. Think of it as a professional presence checklist. No pilot takes off without doing a visual check of the plane to make sure everything is A-OK. No scuba diver jumps off a boat without making sure that the air valves are working. And no business person should walk into a business meeting without the detail check.

The "30-second detail check" before a business meeting gives us the reassurance to concentrate on people and on matters at hand. We don't need to wonder about broken zippers, lunch remnants on our tie, or runs in our hosiery.

Find a restroom and start at the top. Check your hair, teeth, makeup, and earrings. Thousands of women run around all day vaguely aware that they have only one earring on. The other is next to their phone. Secure your scarf or straighten your tie. Check for dandruff, stains, and open buttons. Put your jacket on—buttoned for formality, unbuttoned for a more friendly look. Remember that we are seen far more from the waist up, because we spend much more time seated.

Everything OK? Great. Now you can keep your appointment without distracting doubts about having a piece of spinach caught in your teeth. You'll be able to walk into any room, hold out your hand, and concentrate on the people and business present.

AN ENTRANCE THEY WILL NEVER FORGET

Your "30-second detail check" is complete. The secretary has announced you to your client about fifteen minutes before your appointment because you are working on "Lombardi time." This meticulous coach had all his players set their watches ahead fifteen minutes so that there was an immediate impression of aggressiveness, professionalism, and respect for the other person's time.

You are waiting to be admitted. Don't destroy your first few moments in the client's office by lighting up a cigarette in the reception area, even if they do have ashtrays. Smoke odor on your clothing and breath is an immediate turnoff to a nonsmoking customer.

Don't take a stack of work out of your briefcase, either. This will leave you fumbling and feeling off-guard when the client or his secretary walks in. Read any company newsletters that are available. Take a look at their annual report if it is available. Often if a company has been prominently featured in *Fortune*, *Forbes* or *Business Week*, reprints will be on display.

It is also fine to glance over their file or take out something business oriented, compact, and easily put away. But definitely don't take out a novel to read. A receptionist for a manufacturing firm told me that one vendor was so engrossed in his spy thriller that he never even looked up when two vice presidents came into the reception area to greet him. He stayed engrossed in his book, and they just looked at each other and shook their heads.

Don't spend too much time chatting with the receptionist. Just present your business card, be friendly, and indicate whom you have an appointment with.

Don't eagerly smile at everyone who enters the reception area. Keep a pleasant expression, but stay businesslike and wait for your client to announce him or herself. Then stand up with your briefcase or purse in your left hand and be prepared to shake hands with your right one.

The clock starts when you first make eye contact with the other party. You now have sixty seconds to transform a new acquaintance into a new associate. Or sixty seconds to reestablish your importance to an existing client. There is no need to hurry, rush, or panic. This is the time to demonstrate your control, confidence, and power.

Confident people have a rhythm to their movements and an energy to their stride. Never poke your head around the corner in a tentative gesture. Don't allow the furniture to get in your way or to limit your exposure. If you are told to just go into their office, stand far enough away from the desk so that the person must come from behind it to greet you. If you are the host, it is always more impressive to meet people in the reception area.

Good posture not only takes off ten years and ten pounds, it creates an instant impression of competence. If you get too physically tired at the end of the day, schedule all important face-to-face meetings before 3:00 P.M. Sagging shoulders and slumping posture project subservience, inadequacy, and exhaustion.

Make strong, direct eye contact. One of the best exercises that we do in my seminars is to role play an entrance. For the first entrance, the player makes eye contact, breaks it, and then reconnects for the handshake. This is generally how most of us greet each other.

The second time, the player makes eye contact and maintains it all the way to the handshake. Strength and confidence soar when eye contact is not broken.

MAKING PHYSICAL CONTACT: THE HANDSHAKE

Americans are famous around the world for our fast pace of doing business. In parts of Europe and the Middle East, people may sit for hours over a coffee pot before they even begin to discuss business. In Japan, prospective business associates take weeks just getting to know one other. Even though they will order a confidential report, a Koshinjyo, that gives a detailed account of their potential client, a great deal of time is still invested in developing trust.

Most societies have elaborate rituals for meeting and greeting people, starting with the requirement that you be introduced to a person by someone well known to both parties. Americans move around too much for that. We come from too many different ethnic cultures to rely on the rituals of any one of them. And we are too proud to bow down to anyone. So we shake hands.

The handshake is the focal point of the American greeting ritual, and we have evolved important rules surrounding it. Most of the time, the handshake is the only physical contact that we are allowed in a business relationship. We put a lot of emphasis on it. We often allow impressions based on the handshake and the rituals that surround it to determine the future of a business relationship. For better or worse, those first few moments will often determine the success of your entire meeting.

Shake hands crisply, firmly, and with only one squeeze. Meet web to web, and don't pump up and down more than once. When visiting someone else's environment or office, it is important that you wait momentarily for them to offer their hand. After all, they are the host. If a handshake is not immediately forthcoming, hold out your hand. Never allow an important meeting to start without a handshake.

Don't sandwich the other person's hand between both of yours. It suggests that you are trying to overpower, to patronize, or to lay claim to the higher status. Don't bone crush, glad hand, or wimp out with a two-knuckle finger wiggle, the kind of handshake that only includes half of the hand. Save the limp, dead-fish shake for the selected few who need to know that you perceive them as obnoxious, overbearing, or overly impressed with themselves.

When shaking hands, treat men and women with equal respect. It is as appropriate for a man to offer his hand to a woman as it is for her to offer first. Gender is not a consideration. The shake should be offered as firmly to a woman as to a man.

One of the issues that causes some women discomfort is whether to offer their hand to other women. Traditionally, women have either nodded to each other in greeting or hugged one other. But in most business situations, a firm handshake is the appropriate greeting, never the "little lady finger wiggle."

LET ME PRESENT TO YOU . . .

As you shake hands, take the opportunity to address the other person by name and to repeat your own, "Ms. Carroll, I'm David Jason from United Telephone." Everyone loves the sound of their own name. Repeating it flatters them and helps you remember it. It also gives you a simple way to correct someone else's mispronunciation of your own name.

Use a tag line. Never assume that the people you are meeting know who you are or why you are there. They may have forgotten that a mutual acquaintance sent you. "I'm glad Doug Pepper was able to arrange this meeting. I think you'll find our voice mail system to be exactly what you want."

If there are other people to introduce, remember the golden rule of introductions:

"The Most Honored Person Is Mentioned First"

Gender, age, and even rank are secondary. That means that if you are introducing your boss to a customer, the customer is mentioned first because they are the most important, even if your boss is a vice president and the customer is a junior associate. The introduction would be, "Dan Birdquail, this is my boss, Tom Antlerdance. Tom, Dan is one of my favorite customers and a big fan of our new pantyhose promotion."

When two people of equal rank are introduced, the woman is mentioned first. "Marla Muppet, I would like you to meet Donald Trumpet. Donald has worked in New York for ten years, so you two really have something in common."

When a man and woman are introduced and he is the president of the firm and she is an administrative assistant of that same firm, the introduction would be, "Mr. Landers, I would like you to meet Hilda Britton. Hilda does a wonderful job in our transportation department."

If you simply remember that you honor and give added recognition to the person who is first mentioned, introductions will be easy, connecting, and correct.

ONE MINUTE LATER

That's it. Our sixty seconds are up. Let's take a look and see what has been accomplished.

First, with body language, we have demonstrated that we are comfortable in business situations. We have been surefooted and have avoided potential embarrassment and confusion.

Second, with eye contact and posture we have begun the process of developing mutual trust.

Third, we have demonstrated that being well-organized, on time, and in control of our side of the meeting always elicits respect.

Fourth, we have made someone want to do business with us because everything we have done so far showcases us as a powerful, consummate professional.

PLEASE BE SEATED

Proximity helps create comfort. Many executives have a small, round conference table in their office. It allows them to talk with guests without dominating the "power perch," which is always at the head of the table.

If a conference room is suggested, always direct the meeting there. It is more neutral, like the Geneva, Switzerland, of the business environment. A conference room also has fewer distractions, such as a ringing phone or people popping by.

If the office features a couch and armchairs, select an armchair because a soft sofa is likely to force you into a weaker posture.

If your host stays seated behind a giant desk, just remember my experience with Buck and try to convene to another environment, perhaps the conference room. I have one client that always carries slides with him so he can legitimately request that the meeting be moved into a training room or a conference room where screens and projectors are available.

If your client offers you a beverage, accept it, even if you don't plan to drink all of it. A sip or two simply shows cordiality and friendliness. It also warms the atmosphere and lengthens the meeting. If you are the one offering, make sure you have the coffee available before you suggest it.

One of my clients told me that she went into a prospective client's office and after she accepted an offer for coffee but was turned down because the office was out of it, she agreed to a second offer of cola. The cola was then casually grabbed and drunk by her client. He had turned what should have been a fundamental gesture of business hospitality into a power play. She wisely decided not to share germs.

The awkward moment that comes when you have just sat down, but before serious discussion has started, makes an ideal time to exchange business cards. That practice is standard in Japan. The Japanese never wait until the end of the meeting for the ritual of exchanging cards.

The business card is part of your personal and corporate image. It should always be on excellent card stock, and the image it projects should be professional and in keeping with your industry. Generally black ink on a buff or white card stock is considered the most conservative. Add a gold foil logo, blind embossing, an expertly designed logo, or more than two colors and your card will have more impact. Take the time and spend the money to have new information reprinted. Never give anyone a card with a crossed-out phone number or address. Generally fax numbers belong only on corporate stationary, unless you do a great deal of business by fax.

Avoid listing post office boxes on your card unless you are part of a large and well-recognized company. They give the impression of a company that is not large enough to have a business address.

Exchanging business cards is a good way to bring your new acquaintances "up to speed." The card can impressively present your name, title, and company with no errors. Better yet, the other people at the meeting will usually respond by presenting their cards, too. If someone in the other party has to leave the meeting before the session concludes, exchanging cards early gives everyone the information needed for later follow-ups.

In presenting a business card professionally, don't become over-eager or juvenile. Don't act as though it is the first one you have ever presented. Be smooth—rooting around for one in a purse or brief-case is bad form. Keep your cards in a convenient pocket or have them easily obtainable from your briefcase or card case.

At business meetings it is natural that everyone should have your card. But at cocktail parties, networking sessions, or on airplanes, don't pass your cards around like popcorn. Talk to someone long enough so that you have a sense of whether you want them to be able to locate you. Make your card have value.

SMILE AND THE WORLD SMILES BACK

Try it. Smile. It works because it is almost impossible not to return one. Women usually smile more than men. However, men are learning to smile more because they have discovered how effective it is.

Note that we're not talking about an insipid, artificial grin. A calm, relaxed smile says that you enjoy your work and enjoy meeting people. That kind of smile will put everyone at their ease.

MONKEY SEE, MONKEY DO

Building rapport is the next step in creating a solid first impression. The best technique for building rapport is "matching and mirroring."

We build rapport quickly with those who have manners and mannerisms similar to our own. In fact all Homo sapiens have a built-in mechanism to "ape" others' actions. But this has to be done subtly and with intelligence for it to be effective in the business world.

If someone is calm, slow down and stay controlled, with smoother, less emphatic gestures. Show high spirit and enthusiasm when the other person demonstrates it.

A colleague of mine, Carl Sanders, is a straightforward, hard-hitting, bottom-line bank manager. He is rather traditional in his business manner and is not especially verbal or physically affectionate. When he met Kimberly, a salesperson for a large computer company, she greeted him enthusiastically, pumped his hand, and practically slapped him on the back trying to create instant rapport.

He quickly withdrew. Instead of noting his reaction and responding accordingly, Kimberly moved to fill the awkward silence with nonstop chatter about her company. Within minutes, Carl had decided that Kimberly was not a person he wanted to do business with.

Building rapport starts with the first impression, although you can't expect an instant permanent bond. Only continued exposure will firmly establish trust, respect, and a lasting bond. The objective of the first impression is to start the process on a professional note. You sell yourself first, not your company and not your product.

Finally, nothing destroys a good impression faster than overstaying your welcome. Your exit will be remembered! Wind things up quickly and don't linger.

Part of parting is the follow-up thank-you note. They are incredibly valuable for establishing professional presence because so few people take the time to write them. You will be distinguished from others if you take the time to send them.

I recommend typewritten notes for business as opposed to handwritten ones. One company that I do business with thanks me with "faxed" thank-yous, which is viewed as a bit cut-rate, considering that a fax ties up the customer's telephone lines and uses their paper.

In the note, thank them for their time and consideration. If you have made a great first impression, this will cement it. If things didn't go well, the thank-you restates your case, helps reestablish your presence, and gives a potential client the chance to reconsider.

A NATURAL ATTRACTION

Making an impressive first impression is not fawning over someone, falsely flattering them, or appearing subordinate and submissive. An entrance should create a very human connection that indemnifies all parties. It is a crucial skill in establishing our sense of control and presence.

Part II

◆

GETTING DOWN
TO BUSINESS:
PROFESSIONAL
PRESENCE
ON THE JOB

CHAPTER THREE

THE ART OF SELF-PROMOTION

Self-promotion should not be reserved for the public relations experts, nor for just high-profile business leaders, nor for only billionaire media moguls. Every business professional, if they care about their efforts in business, should make certain they are noted, recognized, and showcased. If properly planned and executed, this isn't offensive hucksterism, it's smart career-pathing.

The Goodwill Games serve as a great self-promotion vehicle for Ted Turner. Malcolm Forbes and Elizabeth Taylor created, in the best sense, a great relationship of mutual self-promotion; whenever they appeared together, the cameras started clicking. Lech Walesa is certainly the highest profile Eastern European leader as a result of his ability to get media attention.

There are many ways for companies to gain respect, market share, and media attention. But individual recognition comes from adept self-promotion. It almost never happens on its own.

That is why it is important to overcome shyness or feelings of inadequacy. Business people generally know more than they realize about their industry. Each of us has a unique perspective and important contributions that deserve to be showcased.

YOU ARE MORE QUOTABLE THAN YOU THINK

When I first moved to Seattle in 1989, I read a humorous column in the *Seattle Post-Intelligencer* about the demise of shoulder pads for women. The otherwise well-informed journalist thought they were ugly and deforming, so he was delighted that they were becoming unstylish.

I sat down and wrote a two-page letter, in a humorous tone, defending shoulder pads as a basic necessity for every woman who is smaller on top than on the bottom, which covers about 99% of us. A week later, on the front page of the Lifestyle section, I saw my name starting off his column.

This was my first step in becoming visible in a brand-new city. The writer had devoted an entire article to the letter I wrote him. Even if I could have bought that much advertising space, it would not have generated as much positive attention and credibility as being quoted by a respected local columnist. It became clear to me that self-promotion isn't as complicated as it appears, and that a large, prestigious publicity machine isn't always necessary.

YOUR FIFTEEN MINUTES OF FAME

Self-promotion is not just the fifteen minutes of fame that Andy Warhol promised us. Self-promotion is much more extensive and useful than that. It is building a good reputation, lobbying for a promotion, as well as positioning ourselves as an authority in our area. The variety of self-promotion methods range from handing out business cards judiciously at a chamber of commerce networking session to being the keynote speaker for a national convention. It's important to choose the kinds of self-promotion that are consistent with our personality and our goals.

EVERYDAY PROMOTION TACTICS

Self-promotion is not just for special times and special projects. Every time we greet people, voice an opinion at a meeting, or take a customer out for lunch, we are promoting ourselves. Here are six things we can do on an everyday basis:

1. Keep agreements and commitments. Nothing makes a more powerful statement of integrity and reliability than doing what we say we're going to do.

2. Keep business cards available at all times. Tuck several in your wallet and suit jacket plus coat pocket and briefcase. When someone asks for information, such as the name of your favorite restaurant in town, jot it down on your business card. Just make sure it isn't dog-eared.

Over thirty million business cards are exchanged every day—it is the most common of self-promotion procedures.

3. Be certain that everyone in your neighborhood, your volleyball or tennis team, your church, and every club that you belong to knows exactly what you do and how to locate you.

To find out that someone you know through one of your organizations placed a huge order with a competing company because they didn't know that you were in that industry is a business tragedy.

This certainly doesn't mean that you should corner your associates at the community swim club with your brochure and flip charts. What it does mean is that you let people know, in a friendly, nonthreatening way, exactly what you do. Asking them what business they are in becomes a fairly easy lead-in to disclose your business as well.

Certainly another way is to offer to do a free seminar or presentation to members of your organization. If you are an image consultant, volunteer to speak to the "Singles' Class" at church about image. If you sell real estate, offer to do a breakfast meeting at the chamber of commerce on buying and selling a home. If you sell athletic equipment and belong to a social club, volunteer to organize a "Sports Day" where you can display your sporting goods.

Members of Rotary Clubs, baseball teams, or the local synagogue will generally do business with people they know personally, *if they know what they do*. There is almost a guarantee that they will get a fairer price and more personal service from a fellow member than from a stranger.

4. Send appropriate letters of congratulations, thank-you notes, and news clippings on topics of interest to clients and colleagues on a regular basis. If you have just had a discussion on a particular stock and the next day there is an article about that company, clipping it out and sending it is a nice way to extend the conversation and your mutual interest.

5. Make business referrals to clients and colleagues whenever possible. If you are comfortable with the caliber of someone's work, allow them to use your name.

One of the most elegant and disarming techniques is to cultivate your so-called competitors, and do cross-referrals with those whom you respect. Your willingness and ability to do this will set you apart from those in your field who come across as insecure and territorial.

(6.) Be accessible. Come early for the social hour prior to an event and don't go racing back to your hotel room after a corporate dinner. Talk, mix and mingle with colleagues and customers. Don't spend the entire evening telling everyone how tightly scheduled and incredibly busy you are and that it is a miracle you even found the time to be here! Make sure you graciously attend company picnics, birthday parties, and after-hours get-togethers. Return phone calls, and if you have moved from one department to another or left a company, stay in contact and be accessible to your former colleagues.

Even well-known people follow the rule of staying accessible. Dr. Joyce Brothers, for example, received a phone call from a small town newspaper in Alabama during an extensive promotional tour where she was interviewed by every major network. Despite her hectic schedule, she took the time, between media appearances, to return the phone call to the newspaper journalist, treating him exactly the way she would have treated an interview from *The New York Times*. She cultivated one more friend in the media, knowing that each reporter adds to the enhancement and credibility of her image and advice.

FALSE MODESTY IS NOT A VIRTUE

It is not good business to wait for others to notice what's going on with you, or to expect others to publicly acknowledge your contributions.

This is especially true for women because research has proven that their accomplishments are less acknowledged and less remembered than those of men.

As a matter of fact, false modesty can be almost as offensive to those you do business with as stepping on others to get ahead. The person who always wimps out and "unselfishly" lets others take the credit for his or her contribution gains little thanks and no respect. When a project is a team effort it is not only possible but necessary to give credit to everyone, including yourself.

If the project requires presentation to a committee, volunteer to be the spokesperson. You will gain status and visibility. If the boss seems to be hoarding all the glory, have a private conversation with him or her and request that you and the other team members have a chance for the limelight, too.

Suggest that photos are taken when you are part of an exciting event. Have the editor of the company newsletter do a front-page story.

When you chair a committee, make sure your name is listed on the program, along with those of the other committee members. If your company has a policy against that, then keep copies of any articles surrounding the program that mention your name.

If you are chairing a project for an organization such as Sales and Marketing Executives or the American Cancer Society, why waste an opportunity to get some name recognition? When it is a project where you are the most important contributor, self-promotion is even more important. In fact, you will look weak and unprofessional if you toil like a workhorse, fully expecting to stay in the background. No one really appreciates a martyr.

A colleague of mine, Pamela Meyers, writes an image column for a monthly newspaper that gives her immeasurable exposure to new clients. She makes copies on glossy paper and mails them to her existing clients as a way to keep in touch. Her columns are informative, straightforward, and offer excellent image information, so they are a great tool for self-promotion.

If you have done a particularly good job with a project for a client, ask for a letter acknowledging that fact. The appropriate time to do that would be when the customer is thanking you in person or on the phone. You might say, "I'm glad it worked, and that you liked the job I did. I'd sure appreciate it if you would put that in writing." Then request that the person send the letter to you, with a copy to your boss or the CEO. Or just ask if you may use them as a reference in the future.

RECOGNITION, NOT NOTORIETY

The right attitude and a sense of perspective are vital to successful self-promotion. So is a sensitivity to how you are perceived by others. No one likes the image of an insatiable publicity hound.

Zsa Zsa Gabor certainly received a great deal of publicity, more than she could ever buy, with her "Cop Slapping" incident. But all it really produced was notoriety. It didn't generate any positive recognition. In fact tee shirts that initially screamed "Free Zsa Zsa" changed to "Kill Zsa Zsa" within a week. Even Zsa Zsa herself said, "I am so famous, it's sickening!"

Self-promotion is not just a "Look How Cool I Am!" attitude. A vendor invited me to his office where he had well over one hundred trophies, certificates, and plaques. Some of them looked as though they had been purchased at a garage sale. Rather than giving him added credibility and visible credentials, the sheer number made him appear shallow and insecure, especially when he insisted on giving me a grand tour.

Several well-placed plaques, or tasteful gifts of recognition, can be a fine addition to a professional's office. Just as we get assurance from a doctor's office where there are impressive diplomas on the wall, we gain a sense of the good citizenship of one whose office displays plaques of recognition from The American Cancer Society, The Salvation Army, the local food bank, or the neighborhood baseball team. But office walls full of plaques or glass cases full of a child's soccer trophies give an indication of a potential ego problem.

Office decor can be useful for self-promotion. Every office needs something that will begin conversation. A collection of wooden ducks or silver spoons, a stunning piece of art, a beautiful wall hanging, or an outstanding view of the city skyline can serve as an initial point of discussion.

Several nicely framed pictures of your family or friends are fine, but avoid unframed snapshots propped up by a pencil holder. A printer, whom our office formerly worked with, had a nude picture with Tom Selleck's head pasted on it. It certainly showed questionable taste.

The familiar or romantic things that work so well in our own home are out of place in an office. A large jewelry box, a lacy picture frame, or a nude statue are too personal. So are alluring pictures of your spouse or personal companion.

Copies of off-color jokes scotch-taped on the wall can be amusing, but they show a lack of concern for other people's sensitivities. One poster quips, "I feel like a mushroom. They keep me in the dark and feed me s———." It may clearly express how you feel about your working environment, but it certainly doesn't set you up as someone on the top of the list for new projects or promotions. Nor does it set the right tone for clients and colleagues.

Make certain your office decor makes a strong statement that is congruent with your business presence and reflects the way you want to be perceived by others.

WRITING YOUR WAY TO SUCCESS

One of the most effective ways to build or enhance a reputation is through the written word. For years, universities and colleagues have insisted on the "publish or perish" doctrine. Although companies don't usually encourage it, they are certainly impressed when employees take the initiative to write and publish an article. It is not necessary to be a professional writer to submit an article for publication, just a competent one who has done the required homework. There are five ways to take advantage of the power of the pen.

1. Volunteer to write a regular column or a quarterly article for your company newsletter. It is a terrific way to become more visible in your company. Those who publish the newsletter will be very grateful, since it is less copy for them to write.

Don't just dash off some remarks off the top of your head. The printed word is permanent and public, so you don't want anything printed that will embarrass you later. Write as well as you can and be sure to check your facts. Have at least two colleagues proofread your article for content, style, and typos. Keep in mind, too, that while a controversial subject or angle may gain you lot of attention, it is likely to alienate more people than it will persuade or impress.

Ask the editor if your picture can be included. Be sure that you have a flattering, professionally photographed, black-and-white head shot on hand.

Inquire when your column will appear and how to secure copies. Watch for its publication and be sure to get extra copies of the published piece to keep for your business portfolio. Just as extracurricular activities are impressive to a college entrance committee, so too are activities that show your talents and motivation to do extra projects.

2. Call your industry trade journal to see if they accept articles from outside sources. If they do, you will have a knowledgeable and captive audience for an article. You will gain important stature within your industry when you appear in a publication that is widely read by your coworkers, your competitors, and your boss.

This exposure helps build your reputation as an expert. From computers to banking to medical care to image consulting, every industry has at least one trade journal where you can showcase your knowledge.

3. Put together a one-page informational piece that your clients would enjoy reading. For instance, if you are in the convention business, you might put together a list of the best restaurants and boutiques in your city. If you sell cellular telephones, compile some amusing customer comments on the unusual ways that their mobile phone has brought them business.

This "newsletter" can be mailed to your existing clients and prospective customers and used as an informational piece for any presentation that you do. Just be sure it is printed on your letterhead and that your name appears.

(4.) When you have been promoted, elected to serve as an officer on a board, or have won an award, type up a simple one-page press release, and send it to your daily newspaper in care of the editor of the business section along with a black-and-white glossy picture. Also send the same release and photo to your weekly business journal. If there are any trade journals that regularly publish information about individuals, be sure to send them a press release, too.

A press release should be done on your letterhead and should look something like this:

For Immediate Release

Contact: Janet Deans
(404)   623-9000

JANET DEANS ELECTED TO MILLION-DOLLAR CLUB FOR HER OUTSTANDING SALES RECORD

Janet Deans was recently made a member of this year's Million Dollar Club for selling over a million dollars worth of real estate in the Atlanta area. She has been with the Ben Bridges Real Estate firm for the past two years and is past president of the New Realtor's Club in Dunwoody. This is the second year that Ms. Deans has won this award.

Ms. Deans will be recognized at the annual awards dinner at the Ritz Carlton on May 12th.

(5.) For maximum exposure, write a book. If that seems overwhelming, then write a booklet in your area of expertise. A booklet can work as an important handout in a company training course or could easily be disseminated at industry trade shows. If your company won't pay for the printing cost, consider investing in the printing yourself. Real estate agents, financial planners, medical personnel, and other service-related professionals will gain a substantial competitive edge with a short, well-written booklet that is chockful of information.

Writing takes time and discipline but the rewards are phenomenal. You will be immediately perceived as an expert in your field. You will have recognizable credibility if you are looking for speaking opportunities, a promotion, or a new job.

A friend of mine in human resources said that he was extremely impressed when he received not only a resume but a copy of the candidate's fifty-page booklet on effective interviewing when he ran an ad for a management opening in his company. Her name was at the top of his list when he set up personal interviews.

MAKING FRIENDS WITH THE MEDIA

Media exposure is the most powerful way to gain attention, credibility, and clout. Whether the interview is with a newspaper or magazine, or you are being featured as an expert on radio or television, the impact and promotional potential are unlimited. When one source finds you interesting, usually others will, too.

Often it is as easy as picking up the phone and calling the editor or a reporter at your daily newspaper. Offer to be interviewed if you have done, or are doing, something newsworthy. When I was involved in a program where we were teaching blind women to apply makeup, a simple phone call to the local newspaper's Lifestyle editor was all it took to get a feature article.

Once you have established a relationship with a journalist, make certain you stay in contact. Drop them an occasional letter, mail them a holiday card, or send an idea for an article with your business card. They will think of you as a valuable person to quote when they are doing a story on robotics, hot-air ballooning, cosmetics, or whatever your specialty is.

To create opportunities for TV appearances, ask colleagues what local news programs they watch. Personally research all network and cable stations to see where the best fit would be for your expertise. If you have an idea, make an appointment with the station manager. The media is constantly looking for ways to keep their scheduling fresh and entertaining.

Barry Henderson, a physician in Atlanta, created an opportunity with a phone call and a subsequent meeting. "Ask the Doctor" was a radio program that ran for one year in Atlanta and brought Dr. Henderson both name recognition and a thriving practice.

To get on local radio programs, listen to see which station has the format that is suitable for what you want to offer. Then call the switchboard of that station and begin your fact finding.

Susan Shulman of Leadership Training Associates, Inc. proposed to a large radio station a series of three-minute informational spots that could be aired during drive time. She interviewed local business professionals about tips for success, and her spots ran regularly during prime time. Getting the best results with the media means that you phone first and connect with a program director, a reporter, or the interviewer on a talk show. Then send information such as newspaper clippings or a sample of your work. You will always get a better response when you have started the relationship on a personal note rather than a mailing.

THEY WANT YOU . . . NOW WHAT?

Once you have danced your way into the hearts and minds of the media, you will probably be terrified of the opportunities you have created for yourself. I can promise that the first time you are on the air, you won't sleep a wink the night before.

The first time I was on a local morning television program, I was so tired from thrashing around all night and worrying that my alarm wouldn't go off at 6:30 A.M. that all I wanted to do was go back to bed. But there I was at the studio with my demonstration items, and they were wiring me with a microphone.

"Three, two, one, you're on," and so I was. I did my first television interview with my pearls clanging against my microphone, my skirt hitched too high, and my clothing demonstration items slipping off the table. Afterward, I watched only once the video of my segment that the station had sent to me. I am no glutton for punishment! But I had certainly learned a great deal for my second appearance, which thankfully did happen.

Whether you are on radio, television, or are being interviewed by the print media, here are six ideas that I have learned over the past ten years of working with the media.

(1.) Narrow the focus of your interview. Decide beforehand what is the most interesting part of your product, your experience, or your company. Don't try to explain everything. It is usually only possible to make one or two points well, unless you are the subject of an extended article or live interview.

(2.) Ask your media contact if they want visuals. Be ready with photos, horizontal slides, or actual demonstration items. "Talking heads" are usually boring, and a photo always adds to any printed articles.

3. Plan your outfit well. Choose blue as your primary color because it is the most photogenic on camera. Before your appearance, sit down in front of a full-length mirror so you will know exactly how you will look in front of the camera. If the station doesn't have a professional makeup artist, hire one yourself. Most television stations will have a list of makeup artists. If not, a phone call to a local professional photographer will produce at least two or three names. If this will be national exposure, hire an image consultant to coordinate your total look. You will be much happier with your appearance.

John F. Kennedy, in his first-ever televised presidential debate, knew the value of looking good. He hired a professional makeup artist and had television training. The results have gone down in media history. Although we probably aren't planning to be presidential candidates, why not learn from those who have been successful on camera?

4. In the printed media, you have little control over what will be printed and how you will sound. Make friends with the interviewer and express your concerns. When I was interviewed over a controversial firing of a female partner in a large accounting firm because of her inappropriate image, I had to be very careful that I expressed myself clearly. Although she was extremely competent and attracted many clients to her firm, she smoked, drank, and swore in front of clients, which her firm deemed unprofessional behavior. Her clothing message was also very masculine.

I clearly asked my interviewers not to distort my viewpoint to make it appear that I was judging this woman without having met her. I wanted to be quoted in a general sense and was not at all comfortable commenting on the specifics of her situation. What I did say was that a powerful image is not gender specific. Smoking, swearing, and exaggerated male or female behavior doesn't enhance anyone's presence. I also said that fair or not, women in business are reviewed more harshly for the exact same behavior that is exhibited in men. In every case, the journalist respected my request to keep my remarks generic and to present a balanced viewpoint.

5. I have found that frankness is refreshing to most journalists, but total candor is a mistake. In the blush of a good interview, I have revealed personal information that later I regretted. I have also found that on TV I didn't have to directly answer every question or accept every suggestion when I instinctively knew it would be a mistake.

One national talk show host wanted me to select people from the audience and critique them on national television. I declined but offered an alternative idea, which was to have the audience critique slides that I had brought to the show.

6. If you generate successful media coverage, and want even more, capitalize on the exposure. Send a copy of the interview or article that featured you plus your background data to other radio stations, TV stations, newspapers, and magazines. If one source has found your expertise worthy of exposure, the others often want to jump on the bandwagon.

SPEAKING UP TO SPEAK OUT

The easiest way to become visible in your company and community is to polish up your speaking skills and speak out! If you have the chance to get up in front of a large group to give a three-minute announcement about an upcoming event, do it. If you have the opportunity to be a speaker at a national sales meeting, retreat, or dinner event, do it. If your company has a public relations firm or a speakers bureau, let them know you are interested in being a company spokesperson in the community.

According to research polls, the greatest fear most people have is the terror of having to speak in public. That is one reason that good speakers are highly valued and well paid. But most of us are not born with speaking skills. This is largely a learned skill that gets better with practice. Toastmasters International, public speaking seminars, and individual training will enhance skills.

No matter where you live, there are dozens of clubs and organizations that use outside speakers on a regular basis. If you have a topic of interest, you can call the program chairperson and ask to address the group. The public library is a good place to find out some of the basic data about local clubs.

Become active in your professional organizations and other business groups. Often these provide opportunities for greater involvement, including public speaking.

Holding a part-time political position is also an effective way to increase your name recognition, while contributing something to your community. Even in a small town, the mayor and the council or school board members have name recognition. Lawyers, doctors, dentists, accountants, insurance and real estate agents, and other business people of all types have advanced their careers through public office.

CREATIVE SELF-PROMOTION

The art of self-promotion has nothing to do with boasting, bragging, or being obnoxious and pushy. The art of self-promotion is simply getting positive attention for yourself, your company, or your pet project with flair and professionalism.

When I worked for a charity organization, I wanted to get the labor unions in Ohio involved in our fundraising. Although they had never been a part of our activities, they were known to be generous, and I decided that I would put my efforts into enlisting their help.

After a dozen phone calls and several business lunches, I found out the name of the key person who could open doors for us. Then I found out what meetings he attended, secured an invitation for myself, and introduced myself to him with a handshake, a business card, and an invitation to lunch the next day.

During our discussion he told me that he had never been personally approached by anyone from our organization. Because of the tremendous number of members he could tap, we had our biggest Walk-a-thon ever. All it took was a little self-promotion.

TAKE THE CREDIT

Take responsibility for getting credit for your accomplishments. In order to be recognized for our efforts we have to self-promote.

Create your own opportunities for media exposure, even if they aren't directly related to your business. If you work for a large company that has its own public affairs department and isn't interested in using you, secure your own spot on local television discussing hobbies like ocean kayaking, home remodeling, or anything else that you have proficiency in. Being noted as a martial arts expert, a proficient Japanese gardener, or a competitive rock climber gives dimension to you professionally and allows other people to recognize and acknowledge you through your outside interests.

Boasting and bragging are not effective self-promotion. But developing a reputation as someone who is willing to get in front of a group, contribute to a newsletter, or talk to the media is effective and powerful self-promotion.

CHAPTER FOUR

EFFECTIVE MEETING MANAGEMENT

Business historians tell us that Henry Ford insisted on being the only person who had a chair at his staff meetings. Everyone else stood. That eccentric technique did more than symbolize Ford's total control over his employees: It also kept meetings with him brief and to the point.

Every day we are blasted with committee meetings, board and staff meetings, department and sales meetings, and team meetings—the list is endless. Meetings have become the black hole of modern business life. They swallow valuable time and energy as voraciously as black holes drink up light.

But part of developing a strong presence is developing a strong meeting style. David Walker, a vice president of a Georgia-based high-technology firm, shared his style with me.

Susan, when I first joined the firm, I told my department heads that I expected our weekly meetings to last no longer than twenty minutes

. . . thirty tops. They all nodded and promptly dismissed the idea. Department tradition had established that ninety-minute meetings were the norm.

At my first early morning meeting, I took off my watch, in kind of a grand gesture, and placed it on the table. After twenty-five minutes had passed, I told my group that the meeting would end in five minutes. Five minutes later, I gathered my papers, said the meeting was over, and walked out.

I left behind a stunned and suddenly insecure group of managers. As I left I said, "Thirty minutes is plenty of time to do everything that's important. It just doesn't allow much time to waste. Let's be prepared next time."

David then sent a one-sentence memorandum the next morning to his entire staff restating his policy. "Our time is much too valuable to spend in repetitive, meandering discussions." His second session ended nineteen minutes after it started and accomplished more specific goals than any of the ninety-minute meetings ever had. No one meandered, no one showboated, and everyone was prepared.

Another of my clients has a company-wide policy of holding three-minute meetings every morning to bring the team together, establish daily goals, and create esprit de corps. The writers of the television series "Hill Street Blues," started each episode with this same abbreviated meeting. Keeping meetings short and sweet establishes a tone of efficiency.

GET TO THE POINT

Successful meetings are brief, focused, and productive. They happen by design, not by inadvertence. The objective of any meeting

is action. Mere ego building and posturing never accomplishes anything productive. True presence helps transform meetings from empty rituals into creative events.

Overly long meetings exhaust energies by extending stressful situations, lengthening detailed discussions, and meandering along without direction. They are also extremely costly. A gathering of eight middle- and upper-management people can cost a company upwards of $700 per hour.

SIMIAN BEHAVIOR

But meetings have other, higher hidden costs. Gathered around a conference table, calm and otherwise rational people tend to function as members of a primitive pack, much like the simian behavior seen in apes and monkeys. Some of these pack instincts are harmless or even amusing, like a young employee trying to act and talk exactly like the boss. Other instinctive behavior, skillfully channeled, is useful. But in the absence of a leader who exhibits strong presence, some of them can interfere with good decision making and polarize groups. Often arising from threats to status or territory, such struggles generate friction and disruptive behavior and force the group into choosing sides.

Yet imitation is a human instinct. Technically it is termed "mirroring and matching." Try this experiment at your next staff meeting. During a lull, casually pretend you are brushing a crumb from the side of your mouth. A few seconds later, do it again.

You probably won't have to do it more than two or three times before the person sitting across the table subconsciously starts to imitate you. It is amazing and somewhat frightening how easily we will imitate other people's behavior, often on a purely unconscious level. Despite centuries of civilization, we humans still instinctively imitate other members of the pack.

Some instinctive imitation helps produce cooperation. Other instincts lead members of the pack to struggle and berate each other, sometimes savagely. As members of a corporate or organization team, we need to understand that the pack mentality is part of our professional context. When we focus its energies and blunt its ferocity, we either keep control of the meeting if we are the leader or maintain our status as an active participant.

For example, if one of the members makes an inappropriate comment such as, "Linda, you are wet behind the ears and your idea is really stupid," the leader of the meeting should immediately react: "Peter, that remark was uncalled for. Let's keep this meeting on a professional level, not a personal one." The leader should not allow the remark to be endorsed or sanctioned by others. The leader should not even wait for others to nod in silent agreement to the inappropriate outburst.

If the leader makes a scathing remark that is completely unfair to one of the participants, a strong, intensely disapproving look back to the leader is appropriate. Also a remark like, "Excuse me, you have that information wrong," is apropos when defending yourself in front of others. A remark like, "I don't think that's fair or accurate. I would like to discuss it with you after the meeting," will help to make certain that you don't lose power and presence.

When the reaction is more nonverbal, like scoffing or rolling of the eyes by other participants when a junior member makes a remark, it is still the responsibility of the meeting leader to address this either verbally or nonverbally. "Is there a problem, John, with Peter's remark?" If the leader doesn't address it or is too intimidated, then the other attendees should make it clear with their offended looks that belittling attitudes are not appreciated and that they are not a part of the same, unjust opinion.

A good leader also publicly apologizes for the deriding remark. "Linda, I'm sorry that remark was made. It was totally uncalled for and we welcome your ideas."

Creating an environment of equality, where all ideas are viewed fairly, requires that the group's energies are focused in positive, productive ways. It is the responsibility of both the leader and each participant.

A VIEW FROM THE HEAD OF THE TABLE

Congratulations on your promotion! Five people hoped to win that job, but the company picked you. For three years you've been telling your spouse how much time the company wastes in meetings. Now it is time to call *your* staff together.

Incidentally, all four disappointed candidates will be waiting to see how you do. They have all shaken your hand and congratulated you. Now they are sitting back and hoping that you will fall flat on your face. Instead, impress them with your professional presence.

First, send out a short memo prior to the meeting that targets, in one sentence, each point you want to discuss. This allows each attendee to be prepared with suggestions and new ideas. It also shows that you, as the leader, have clearly thought through the agenda and are not wasting anyone's time.

Second, know everyone's name. You will have much more presence if you can call on every member using their first name. Also, if a superior or outside person is attending the meeting, don't embarrass them by making them struggle with new, unfamiliar names. Use large tent cards placed in front of each attendee with their first name in large letters.

Third, understand what each person does so that you won't inadvertently step on toes. If you defer to someone else's advice, make sure that the advice is coming from the most-qualified and well-recognized individual in the group.

Fourth, be careful about personal comments, even those intended as "only kidding," unless you know the group very well. I once chaired a meeting where I made the off-handed comment, "Don't schedule a meeting during George's nap time." Although it was common knowledge that George took a short nap every day after lunch and despite the fact I made the remark in good humor, George was mortified.

My thoughtless comment was not meant as a personal attack. George, however, saw my comment as an assault on his virility and endurance. Despite my instant and sincere apology, that one careless, public statement eroded our relationship until I had the time to smooth things over.

I should have known better. Masculinity, femininity, age, weight, baldness, visual acuity, height, and other physical or emotional attributes may be topics for banter among good friends. But with the possible exception of that peculiarly popular event known as the "roast," they are not appropriate for public comment in a business meeting.

Fifth, make certain that the meeting doesn't disintegrate into a lot of technical jargon that only a few attendees understand. It is up to the leader to clarify information and to make sure that confusion isn't written on the faces of the members.

A TALE OF TWO STYLES: CONFLICT AND CONSENSUS

FIRST, CONFLICT

It is common, these days, for young executives to have older subordinates—people who may have been passed over for promotion or simply declined them because they didn't want to move. Douglas Girt was a confident twenty-nine-year-old Wharton MBA hired directly by the CEO of an engineering firm. Doug was full of great ideas. He felt he knew just what the company needed.

Andrew, who had dotted-line responsibility to Douglas, had been with the company since it was formed twenty years ago. Rather than get Andrew on his side, Doug decided to show him his thinly veiled contempt at the first staff meeting.

He ignored the fact that Andrew had a long-term relationship with many employees. Their loyalty remained with Andrew. Doug, being new, had the title and authority, but had yet to earn the respect of his staff. With diplomacy and skillful management, he could have earned that respect and made an ally of Andrew. He could have deferred to Andrew at least once during each meeting without losing the respect of the group. He could have shown a little humility and said something like, "I certainly have some big shoes to fill." Instead he chose confrontation at the staff meeting.

By his initial lack of respect, Douglas inevitably started a chain reaction. Andrew and his supporters began to mutter among themselves at the meeting. They started quietly sabotaging every new idea outside the meeting.

In response, Doug got tough. He made his orders clear. In subsequent meetings, he physically moved around the table, telling Andrew and the others exactly what he expected of them . . . indeed, what he demanded of them. He had a visible revolt at every meeting, not in words, but in nonverbal behavior that included slouched posture, hands behind the head, and meaningful glances among the members.

SECOND, CONSENSUS

Skilled leaders do not have to demand what they want from their groups. They demonstrate it. I have seen this principle practiced by experienced meeting managers throughout the country.

Martin R., producer of a popular television show, is among the best I have ever seen at obtaining a consensus. I attended one of his meetings as a consultant. I watched, fascinated, as he brought a group of writers and VIPs into agreement on a hotly controversial issue: whether or not to replace the co-star of a popular series.

In the process, Martin said little and never expressed any demands. He occasionally reminded the group about budget constraints, production lead times, and other casting considerations. When the group started to digress, Martin brought them back to the topic at hand. Each member of the group spoke at least once; all expressed strong opinions. Their final decision, determined by consensus, was completely in accord with the producer's position.

"Congratulations, Martin," I said to him in private, on the way to the airport. "You finally got everyone's unanimous support for a star they wanted to fire. You are a born leader!"

"Not really, Susan. They are all intelligent people and they want the show to stay on top of the ratings," he told me. "I just gave them the facts. I kept the meeting focused, didn't take sides, and let them reach the appropriate conclusion themselves."

He left unsaid that he had also respected everyone's territory and status, and he made certain that everyone contributed to the outcome. With that foundation, he had only to focus their energies, preserve their sense of purpose, and summarize the prevailing viewpoint at the conclusion. By safeguarding each member's status as an individual, he was able to rely on commitment to team goals.

FIFTEEN WAYS TO MASTER A MEETING

The concepts of handling a meeting professionally are sometimes subtle and often challenging. To be effective, they must be expressed and reiterated in concrete, tangible ways.

The following list is drawn from the experience of a number of highly successful meeting managers, people like Martin. Their ideas and suggestions will advance your meeting mastery and help develop your professional presence.

FIFTEEN WAYS TO MASTER MEETINGS

1. Reserve the most impressive, appropriately appointed conference room when the meeting warrants it. It will immediately add stature to your session.

2. Make certain that there is no debris left from the previous occupants. Chalk boards and marker boards should be erased and

clean. Extraneous flip charts should be removed. Coffee cups and refreshment remnants should be gone. Make sure that community cleanup is part of how you end your meetings.

(3) If you serve refreshments, have them available at the conference table and on a self-serve basis. Don't waste time by allowing your people to mill around the coffee pot.

(4) Provide a written agenda and stick to it. Even if the agenda lists only a few items, it will show you to be an organized, directed leader. Be careful. Allowing too much digression from the agenda detracts from your professional presence.

(5) Never recap information for latecomers. They can learn everything they need from someone else later. Your recapitulation represents tacit approval of their tardiness.

(6) Stand up when you want to make an especially important point. Standing up makes you at least twice as tall as anyone else in the room. It reinforces your position and authority.

(7) Don't rush. You want to keep the meeting upbeat and moving swiftly, but if you speak too quickly you will appear insecure and frightened. The "pregnant pause" is good drama and a highly effective attention-getter.

(8) Observe your audience. Watch their body language. Are they confused? Stop and ask questions. Find the source of their puzzlement and resolve it. Are they bored? Revive their active participation by asking specific questions.

(9) Control your hands. Don't click pens, fold and unfold paper. Keep your wrists firm when gesturing. Always keep your hands on the table and visible.

(10) Keep facial expressions positive and attentive. Others are likely to imitate both your expressions and your attitudes.

(11) Make strong, connected eye contact with each person at the meeting. Don't move on until you know the color of their eyes. Don't

just sweep over the group and then bury your nose in your notes. And don't ignore people at the end of the table.

(12) Never accept telephone calls during a meeting. Don't allow people to walk in and out of your meeting, or to pop in, even for "just a second." If you do, the meeting loses its momentum, the attendees lose their concentration, and you lose your professional presence.

(13) If you have to leave a meeting early, be certain to clearly explain when you must leave and why. It shows respect for all attending members. Abrupt leave-taking without an explanation will significantly diminish all the previous progress.

(14) Be careful about overdoing clichéd sports-oriented terms to energize a group. Most women and some men find it tiresome and not at all inspiring. Too many coaching analogies like "Let's score a touch down on that one, guys," or "We need to run a pass with our star quarter back" are dated and irritating.

(15) For meetings longer than one hour, allow sufficient bathroom, refreshment, smoke and stretch breaks. One manager, who heads a public relations firm, has his employees line up facing in one direction, like spoons. Then he puts on some jazzed-up music and each person gives the person in front of them an invigorating back rub. Then they turn in the other direction and give the person who just gave them a back rub one in return. It is not a technique for all offices, but it works well as a rejuvenator in his free-spirit environment.

BREAK IT UP

There is one other valuable technique for managing a meeting with powerful presence. It is one that I learned when I served on a jury. Throughout the course of the trial, the twelve of us in the jury unintentionally formed several small cliques. Forbidden to discuss the trial, we still formed friendships with other jurors who seemed to share the same values, background, work experience, and ideas. When we moved into the jury room for deliberations, alliances were forged that had started forming in the lunch room.

Fortunately, our jury was headed by a capable and wise woman. After three hours of futile haggling, she called for a break. When we returned, she had arranged place cards with our names on them in front of different seats. By breaking up our comfortable seating arrangement, she broke up our connection with the clique.

One hour later, we had settled the case and I had learned an important new aspect of professional meeting management. Breaking up comfortable, established seating arrangements often breaks up obstructive alliances.

THE POWERFUL PARTICIPANT

You may recall that the wizard Merlin won a prominent place in myth and legend by advising King Arthur to seat his knights at a round table. The world's first expert on group dynamics, Merlin theorized that a round table would blur inter-knight status distinctions. He was right, and the principle is still valid today.

Unfortunately, most modern conference rooms feature rectangular tables. Such clearly defined space triggers territorial instincts and exaggerates differences in rank. That is why only the person who called the meeting may sit at the head of the table. The head of the table is the "power perch." It is reserved for the most senior person present. The three other important positions are those to the right of the power perch, the seat to the left, and unless it is too far away, the seat opposite.

If you are new to the organization and uncertain about your place at the table, hover around the coffee and doughnuts, examine the conference room's paintings, or admire the view. Better yet, take the opportunity to review your notes or to greet others standing in the room. Wait to learn the seating protocol from more longtime attendees and then take your seat.

If you are seated when an important person enters the room, stand up to shake hands. For the past four thousand years standing up to acknowledge someone has been a show of respect. It still is today. And a woman should rise as readily to her feet as any man.

Here are some additional guidelines that will help you move to the head of the table while clearly showing your support for your boss.

- Sit as close to the leader as protocol permits. With physical proximity, you demonstrate an implied closeness in ideas and values.

- Follow the leader. Without looking like a mime, "mirror and match" the energy level of your superior. Also, if the leader uses formal conduct and speech, so should you. Keep in mind that this rule has its limits. The leader can sit on the corner of the table and appear confident and relaxed. If you do the same thing, you will appear disrespectful and insubordinate.

- Respect the leader. No daydreaming and no private, off-stage conversations with neighbors. If your boss is engaging in other conversation when you are making a presentation, you can either ignore it if it isn't lengthy, or simply stop talking and ask if they have a specific question.

I once presented a seminar to about twenty-five people where the gentleman who hired me talked to his zone manager the entire time. I finally stopped talking and, with as much good humor as I could muster, asked them, "Am I missing out on something, gentlemen?" They both replied, "Oh, no, we were just talking about how great this seminar is." It was a welcome response, at least to me, but more importantly, they refrained from their discussion for the rest of my presentation.

- Discuss, but don't argue. When a leader has to constantly take time to break up fights, time is wasted and reputations are tarnished.
- Sit erect and square your shoulders. Posture provides the context for everything you say. Sitting up with squared shoulders makes you look fit, vital, and alert. Keep your arms on the table. Lean forward slightly with a bit of an angle to your head when you want to express interest. Moving physically closer, even slightly, increases the sense of involvement.
- Don't create subconscious barriers to communications. Be especially careful if you are in the habit of folding your arms across your chest.
- Demonstrate high energy and involvement. A high-energy level is contagious. It is extremely appealing and a valued quality in a team player.

TAKE A STAND

There is another aspect to being a powerful participant. Speak out! Take a stand! Sound off! Sometimes it is worth taking a calculated risk at a meeting because a confident leader likes to see a certain strength of conviction. But taking risks requires that you do your homework. Don't spout off unless you know exactly what you are talking about and it doesn't directly contradict what the leader has just said.

Know, too, that introducing anything controversial will create tension. However, tension and a bit of rowdiness, can produce innovative ideas as long as they are clearly summarized.

If a boss is rude to you during a meeting, you have two options. You can either confront the remark as soon as it is made or make certain that you meet immediately in private to discuss the contemptuous treatment. If you let it slip by, if a pattern develops, not only will your boss lose respect for you, you will lose respect for yourself.

Meetings are a good place to showcase and self-promote. If you have developed a great idea for a new product or promotion, bounce it off a few trusted colleagues before bringing it before a larger group. It is better to think through a plan and revise it or even get it totally shot down with some loyal friends than to misspeak in front of a larger, more public group.

VALUABLE OPPORTUNITY

Meetings are a central part of communication and cooperation within any organization. Do not think of them as drudgery. Recognize, instead, that they present valuable opportunities to develop skills and build a reputation, as well as to stay on top of essential company information. Whether as a powerful leader or participant, skillful meeting management will win widespread recognition and respect for your professional presence.

CHAPTER FIVE

TAKING CHARGE THROUGH NONVERBAL COMMUNICATION

Cori Cutter, a Seattle salesperson, set out to convince a seasoned mortgage banker that the title insurance company she represented was worth taking a chance on. Although Cori was young, she had learned to listen intently, to validate information through effective body language, and to keep her answers brief and reassuring.

As the banker described the complex issues and his concerns, he stopped suddenly and said, "Can you handle all of this, Cori? There's a lot of politics involved, a lot of egos, and frankly I'm not sure you have the experience to manage my accounts."

Rather than getting defensive, rather than jumping in and acting overeager, or talking the issues to death, Cori stayed calm and friendly. She looked the older man squarely in the eye, and, after a brief pause, simply said, "No problem. I can handle it."

If Cori had reviewed her excellent credentials or her experience at great length, she would have appeared defensive. Cori knew that the banker was aware of her background, and she *read* that what he was looking for was reassurance. Cori used six simple words, delivered with powerful body language, to give him what he wanted. She created assurance, established presence, and took charge.

DON'T COMPLAIN, DON'T EXPLAIN

The manager or sales professional who wants to be perceived as having power and presence seldom wastes time overexplaining, apologizing, or justifying opinions. Brief, decisive statements delivered with authoritative body language, remain one of the most effective ways to gain a desired result.

UP CLOSE AND PERSONAL

Doing business in person provides us with a combination of physical, intellectual, and sensory clues. That's why people fly thousands of miles for a one-hour meeting. Otherwise we would just trade videos, or rely solely on tele-conferencing. Although both of those methods do help to facilitate business decisions in our age of technology, we ultimately need the reassurance of personal presence.

We need not only to hear and see those with whom we do business, we need to be in their presence to use all our senses to ascertain whether or not we trust them. We need to shake their hands, look them in the eye, see how they move their bodies, and check out how comfortable we feel around them.

An individual always has more prestige in person. That's why people wait hours to get tickets to a concert when they already own the compact disc, or stand in line at the bookstore to meet a well-known author and get an autograph. That's why people brave the weather and the crowds to get a glimpse of the president, or the pope, or the latest celebrity. That is why presidents and high-level executives of companies generally stay accessible to their employees. Being able to say you saw, or better yet touched or talked to a person with power or presence confers a kind of prestige by association. In addition, it is much easier to influence others and exert status in person.

UNSPOKEN POWER PLAYS

In the movie *Shock to the System*, starring Michael Caine, the individual with the perceived power and presence gets his cigar lit. As power shifts back and forth between Michael Caine and his nemesis, they take turns lighting each other's cigar. It became a clear visual signal as to who was in charge.

In the business world, the one with the lesser amount of power does the lighting of the cigar, the pulling out of the chair, the hailing of the cab, and all the other subtle and not so subtle things that define the differences between the subordinate and the superior.

When it comes to physical contact such as a slap on the back, a reassuring hand on the arm, or a friendly wing around the shoulder, the one with the greater amount of power and presence initiates the touch. They are *allowed*, for instance, to reach over and give a reassuring pat on the back to a distraught colleague. They are also *allowed* to walk into a subordinate's office and pick up photographs and comment on them.

When the reverse happens, however, and a less-positioned person grabs the forearm of the chairman in the hallway to get his attention, it is a corporate faux pas of the highest magnitude. It is almost always inappropriate for a subordinate to initiate physical contact or casually pick up items in a boss's office.

SENDING NONVERBAL MESSAGES TO COLLEAGUES

Feeling empowered and appearing assured on the job includes handling those people who seem to have nothing better to do than to fritter away your time. One of the most common complaints of both managers and salespeople is the time wasters who stroll in and hang around to chat. How can you minimize the amount of extra time that people spend in your office?

Use a straightforward solution. Stand up. If you are seated and busy and someone walks into your workspace and you don't want the interruption, stand up and stay standing. It is difficult for visitors to plop down and feel comfortable if you remain standing. They will generally get to the point and leave. Then you can sit down and get back to work. If they don't get the hint soon enough, you can pick up a file folder and move toward the door.

Dealing professionally with intrusions means that no one ever feels dismissed. Skillfully using less obvious methods means that you don't have to resort to the not so subtle glance at your wristwatch, or drum your fingers on the desk. You are acknowledging the person and giving your full attention.

TELLING LIES

It is impossible to give assurance and take charge when we are being lied to. Of course, lying occurs millions of times each day in thousands of companies; white lies, corporate lies, guilty lies, jealous lies, lies about why someone was late, or about how we spent the weekend. Sometimes telling a lie can be a kind and considerate act, created to save someone embarrassment. At other times it wreaks havoc on both personal and professional relationships.

Playing poker is an extraordinary way to get feedback on how you tell lies and how adept you are at reading other people's. Holding a losing hand and pretending you will win the pot requires superb nonverbal skills. You will learn quickly if you are a good liar and also how well you discern when others are lying to you. Being able to size up the other players' body language, detect changes in posture, eye contact, and anxiety levels and ultimately determine if they are telling the truth will help you win in poker. The skills are the same in the business world.

Although it is fairly easy to lie verbally, it is much more difficult to be completely convincing in a falsehood since our nonverbal behavior gives us away, and nonverbal evidence is always more believable.

When a coworker rolls her eyes, grimaces and says, "I love

the new vacation policy," the obvious message is that she doesn't. When an associate sighs, heaves his shoulders, shoots a dark look and says, "Of course, I don't mind working late," he would rather not.

There are ten specific signals to look for when someone is not telling you the truth. No single gesture by itself indicates that someone is lying. But if you see several of these together, be wary of the verbal message.

1. There is an incongruency between what is said and how it is said. If someone replies, "No problem, I don't mind if you smoke," in a very low voice while looking pained, the truth is that he or she does mind if you smoke.

2. The person fails to maintain strong eye contact and instead looks at the floor, or the ceiling, anywhere but at you.

3. The same information is repeated several times. The repetition is an attempt to make it sound truthful.

4. The voice is higher-pitched and louder than normal. This is an involuntary, often fearful, reaction.

5. The eyes shift, generally to the left. In studying the classic Kennedy-Nixon televised debate, Kennedy's eyes rarely wavered, while Nixon's blinked or shifted constantly. Those who listened on the radio to the debate, felt that Nixon was the more credible. Those who watched it on television, determined that Kennedy appeared more trustworthy.

6. The pupils of the eye become smaller. Generally people telling the truth have larger pupils. Tiny pupils are sometimes an involuntary response by the body to a deliberate falsehood.

7. The person swallows harder and more obviously. Again, this is an involuntary physical response.

(8) The face is flushed and perspiring.

(9) The person speaks at a different rate of speech than normal, generally much faster.

(10) A hand is placed in front of the mouth when information is given, in an attempt to muffle the words.

DEALING WITH THE LIAR

There are several ways to handle a liar. The direct approach is often best. "Sharon, this sales report is wrong. I know you didn't sell to Federated because your expense report didn't include a trip to New York, and I know they don't place orders over the phone." Then watch for any of the above signals in her behavior.

If her nonverbal signals confirm your suspicions, then, while keeping eye contact, confront her with an open-ended question such as, "Can you explain this?" Wait silently, maintaining strong body language, for her response.

If it is clear through nonverbal information that your boss is lying to you, determine the magnitude of the lie and how it directly affects you. Is it just a facesaving device for the boss and rather harmless as far as you are concerned? Or are you being compromised and sabotaged?

You will feel powerless and victimized if you are genuinely threatened by the lie and elect not take some action. If your boss says, "Don't worry about your job. Even with this merger, your position is not in jeopardy," but is unable to give you eye contact or any other signs of assurance, take verbal action. Respond with, "I don't feel that you are being straight with me. What are my chances of surviving the cuts?" will return some power and control to you.

Our ability to discern what is really being "said" and where the truth lies is simply our attuned instinct, and generally it will prove to be authentic.

GETTING TO THE TRUTH

If someone has pretended to feel one way while influencing others in the opposite direction, clarification is in order. "Michael, you clearly supported my position on not shipping to delinquent accounts. Now I hear that you don't think our salespeople should worry about whether an account has been paid or not before shipping them more goods. What *is* your position?"

The concern here is that attitudes and private conversations, not verifiable facts, comprise the deceit. But that doesn't mean that clear duplicity should be ignored. As competent professionals, we need to know who is on our side and who isn't. Once we are clear on the caliber of the lie, we have three options:

(1) Sit down and directly confront the liar, carefully reading all signs of body language. If the lie is readily admitted to, graciously close the matter if it is in the best interest of the company, but don't forget the occurrence.

(2) If you don't know exactly who the liar is, plan a strategy to discreetly find out who may be undermining you. Without direct confrontation, many times the root of the problem becomes apparent and no fingers are pointed in the process.

For example, if you find out that one of your employees has clearly been lying to the vice-president about your treatment of your staff, careful questioning of the vice-president can reveal who the employee is.

Watching his reaction to a nondefensive question like, "By the way, did you have lunch with Jerry this week?" can confirm suspicions or eliminate possibilities. Then you can follow up with a more straightforward question like, "I feel that I am being undermined by Jerry. Can we discuss it so that all the cards are on the table? Would you tell me exactly what Jerry has told you about personnel issues in my department?"

3. The third option is to try to rise above the lie, to show class and dignity because the lie is unfounded and clearly unbelievable. Unfortunately, if the same lie is told enough times, it begins to have the ring of truth. Although there is a certain amount of complicity assigned to those who don't defend themselves, staying silent is always a choice.

THE POWER OF SILENCE

One of the things that most of us have learned in business is that it takes much more than the *spoken word to convince us*. The flip side is that it takes more than the *spoken word to get what we want*. That is why the appropriate use of silence is an important skill to master.

When we talk too much, we will eventually give away too much information. But because we live in such a heavily stimulated environment, silence is both unfamiliar and uncomfortable. When we rush in with chatter to fill the void, we can lose control of the encounter.

Al Marchman, a talented attorney and negotiator, delivers appropriately placed silence. He rarely immediately responds to any important question; the pregnant pause gives him a chance to reflect. Often the other person quickly fills up the silence by continuing on, which gives Al unintended but very useful information, which he can use effectively.

In the corporate world the person who does all the talking is not necessarily the one with the upper hand. Business transactions prosper when the power of silence is both understood and judiciously used. Making your point forcefully may not be as important as staying quiet long enough to hear what points someone else wants to make. The individual who talks all the time and seldom gives others an opportunity to speak is often resented and gets a reputation as a blowhard or windbag.

The use of silence to encourage prospective employees to reveal more than they had planned has long been used by the savvy interviewer. However, the most powerful use of silence is in focused listening, neither thinking about what you are going to say next, nor scheming about how you will convince the other person. Focused listening requires mental concentration and physical alertness. Giving someone your undivided attention, acknowledging that person with nods and other nonverbal encouragement, being patient and not interrupting creates an atmosphere of trust. Even if the subject is routine, don't let your mind wander. The better listener in any encounter will end up with more information, and information is power.

Taking notes is a silent form of flattery in the business world. Noting that what someone has said is worthy of a more permanent record shows your respect.

SOFT POWER

Claire Olson, a Cleveland business owner, is an example of someone who effectively uses what I term "soft power." "Soft power" is knowing you are in control, but rarely ever having to flaunt it. Influence over others is gained in a less confrontational, more friendly and direct manner.

In board meetings, Claire seldom says much until the meeting is well in progress. What she does, instead, is to keep such focused, positive attention on whoever is talking that most of the participants end up addressing their arguments and concerns to her side of the table.

Her well-timed and limited verbal contributions enable her to influence the direction of the board much better than if she contributed verbose, unfocused chatter. When she does talk, others listen. Her "soft power" approach involves weighing each contribution until she has heard from everyone and then summarizing the best of the contributed information along with her own point of view.

WHAT WE BELIEVE

There are many ways to give and receive information. But the most powerful statements come from well thought out information endorsed by unwavering, direct, and focused body language. Nonverbal communication supports and validates all our verbal information and it is always more believed that anything we say.

CHAPTER SIX

YOUR ELECTRONIC PRESENCE

Although face-to-face meetings have been the basis for business relationships for centuries, the ubiquitous power of technology has put a new face on professional presence. Strong relationships can be built on the strength of our electronic presence.

Voice mail, facsimile machines, car phones, and conference calling are exciting enhancements that can add credibility to our business dealings. So is good telephone etiquette.

VOICE MAIL—CAN WE TALK?

A machine answering your phone used to be the mark of a small, one-person office. Large offices always had a live presence. Answering machines were unthinkable . . . until someone decided that a jazzed-up version would probably be a wonderful enhancement to a receptionist.

Voice mail is this decade's answering machine. It is truly an efficient way to transmit valuable business information. When we look at the statistic that indicates that only 30% of phone calls are ever completed on the first try, voice mail becomes a much more efficient way to talk.

But it is efficient and desirable only when paired with a live person who answers the phone first and then offers to direct you to voice mail if your party is unavailable. When customers initially call in, it is rude and unprofessional to have a system that requires them to spend time listening to recordings and punching buttons before they ever hear a human voice.

Here are twelve tips so that voice mail won't backfire:

1. The best messages are short ones no matter whom you call. If you are leaving messages for your boss, it is even more important to keep them short and sweet. Remember that a boss often has to listen to daily reports from all personnel, which may require nearly an hour. Keep your correspondence to the point and win points with your boss.

2. If you must leave a lengthy message, be sure to play it back for accuracy. Many systems will allow you to erase it and start over if you don't like what you said or how you said it.

3. Never leave a harsh, negative message on voice mail. You may regret it later, and unlike a conversation, the receiver can play it over and over and even redirect it to other people. You may even have a conciliatory conversation prior to the recipient retrieving the message. Then when the message is played back later, it leaves a very sour note.

4. Don't record anything that can be misinterpreted or is very confidential. Voice mail can be stored and come back to haunt you.

5. If you are a manager sending out information to your staff, don't read preprepared memorandums or announcements over the phone. If you are going to do that, why not just fax it? Reading information negates the value of using voice mail. Use notes if you have to, but keep your voice friendly.

6. Always be ready to leave a message. Seventy percent of the time the person you want to speak to will not be there. Jot down bullets of important information so you won't ramble.

7. Don't be flippant in your messages. You may be doing it in jest, but Linda Ellerbee was fired from her job as a television writer when she pressed the wrong button and sent out a very sarcastic message to every newsdesk in the country.

8. Be sure to check your voice mail at least twice a day and more if you receive time-sensitive information.

9. Don't leave messages from noisy restaurants, bars, or parties. Background noise will be heard loud and clear. You can even purchase and play audio tapes that sound just like a busy office if you want to acquire some authenticity.

10. If you want to really impress a boss or client, leave messages at 6:00 in the morning or late at night.

11. To cover all your bases, leave two messages: one with a living, breathing body, i.e., the receptionist or secretary, and the other with an accurate, mechanized machine.

12. Compliments are one of the nicest messages to receive on voice mail. No one ever resents a kind word. Surrounded by directives and demands, a kudo is a welcome oasis.

CREATING DRAMA

Many business people have developed a strong, hard-hitting style by using fax correspondence almost exclusively. Rather than picking up the phone, they hit the keyboard. Rather than making a request, they create urgency.

Sending a fax has more drama than a letter. It feels more like a hand-delivered telegram. You can also do it on your own time because with facsimile you don't need the luxury of both people being available at the same moment.

To protect your information if anything is of a confidential nature, don't send a fax, unless it is a one-person office, or the person receiving the message will be right next to the machine. Fax is just like mail, but without the envelope.

YOU CAN'T BLUFF

One of the powerful aspects of faxing is that you can't bluff. Prior to facsimile machines, when you asked someone if they had your contract ready and they answered yes, you could either expect it the next day if they used express service, or in several days if they mailed it. There was a hedge factor, a procrastination inherent in the ways that information used to be sent.

Today if you ask someone if the contract is ready and they answer yes, you say, "OK, then fax it." Talk about presence! It is almost like being there and standing over their shoulder. Faxing has enabled us to create powerful presence even in remote locations.

A REMOTE LOCATION

Sending a fax from a remote location will add a certain urgency and importance to your information. Often, sending a fax to a client from the airport or a business center is a better way to reschedule a meeting than a phone message. Faxing is an effective way to create a strong presence without being present.

You know that your information will be absolutely accurate if you write it and fax it. Just be sure to call the client's office to alert them that a facsimile is on its way.

Take cover and transmittal sheets with you if you will be faxing on the road. Having transmittal sheets with your company's name and logo will help maintain your image if you fax from a remote location.

THE FAX, MA'AM, JUST THE FAX

Cartoon transmittal sheets for facsimiles are fun for inner-office correspondence but only when the information sent is neutral or positive. A negative message accompanied by a fatuous transmittal sheet is not smart. Another "not smart" move is to use silly transmittal sheets for traditional client correspondence. It will diminish both your presence and your message.

A popular way to use facsimile machines is to send jokes and comics. This is one method of establishing rapport with another department, but just be sure that your company doesn't take a dim view of it.

One of my clients who is in sales told me that she constantly fights with the distribution center over her late shipments. She decided that her relationship with them was at an all-time low and that they viewed her as a real pain in the neck, so she changed tactics.

She built her presence with them by faxing the director funny cartoons, often with self-deprecating remarks about herself or about salespeople in general. She turned around a hostile relationship and won their support. And she attributes this to the effective use of her electronic presence.

WITHOUT A POSTAGE STAMP

It is fine to send compliments, personal and professional recognition, and general warm, fuzzy information by fax. Just don't use it to send thank-you notes or condolences. The quality of the paper and the printing isn't conducive to a sincere thank-you for a gift or to heartfelt concern over an injury or death.

THE VOICE OVER THE PHONE

Disc jockeys sound so cheerful over the air because they have mastered the technique of smiling while announcing information. Smiling on the phone will affect the quality of your voice. You will sound bright, friendly, and positive. Standing up while talking on the phone will create lively, energetic communication.

The correct way to call someone is to identify yourself first, your company second, and then request to speak to the specific individual. Beyond that, here are tips from A to Z.

Phone Tips from A to Z

A. Make telephone appointments for important calls to discuss matters in depth, just as you would make person-to-person appointments. Being on someone's calendar at 3:00 P.M. on Tuesday will give you, your phone call, and your information almost the same level of importance as an in-person meeting.

B. Never leave your phone number when the person you are calling doesn't know you and has no idea why you called. You will probably never receive a phone call back, and that puts you at a disadvantage when you call again.

However, do leave your name and a brief message. Even without leaving your phone number you can start building a relationship with the receptionist or secretary so that your message will be passed on promptly, even perhaps with a nice remark about you.

C. Don't act offended when the receptionist asks, "Will she know what this is regarding?" The question may sound condescending, but busy executives receive scores of calls a day and often need a memory jog.

D. When calling medium to large corporations, always identify yourself and your company, even if you have called many times before. Unless you have a distinctive voice or accent that is instantly recognized, and you are certain to get the same receptionist, you can get off to a bad start if you are mistaken for someone else.

E. If you call small firms regularly, judge when it is time to drop your company name and just give your first and last name.

F. If you are repeating the same information on the phone that you have said many times before, take a tip from professional speakers who often say the same thing two hundred times a year, and make sure it is fresh. It may sound stale to you, but don't let it sound jaded and turned into monotone mush.

G. Never get irritated with a secretary because the boss is consistently unable to take your phone call. If you lose your presence with the secretary, you probably will get a bad review when your message is passed on.

H. If your calls are not being taken, ask when the best time is to return calls, but don't whine about it.

I. Your voice will sound happier, your manner will be more relaxed, and your presence will zoom when you concentrate phone work on Thursdays and Fridays. People are much more receptive to phone calls closer to the weekend.

J. Never say, "How are you today?" unless you know the person you have called and genuinely care how they are. Otherwise, you will be immediately written off as another telephone solicitor.

K. Make bullets of information so that you are certain to cover all important points.

L. It is always easier to say "no" over the phone than in person. If the decision is important, request a meeting because we are always more powerful in person. If what you hear isn't what you expected, you will be able to negotiate better in person for your Plan B.

M. Even though you have introduced yourself to the receptionist, reintroduce yourself to the person you are calling so that there are no mixups.

N. Don't call clients by their first name on the phone until a relationship has been established.

O. Never say, "Is this a good time to call?" when phoning someone you don't know. You will sound weak and wishy-washy, and it is never a good time to talk to someone you don't know. However, it is considerate when both parties are well acquainted and the conversation will take more than fifteen minutes.

P. When you do know the person well, and the phone conversation is certain to be lengthy, offer the courtesy of scheduling a phone meeting at a later time. You will both be better prepared.

Q. "Call waiting" is often the only way for a one-person firm to do business. But if you have initiated the call to a client, think twice about putting that client on hold while you take another call. If you do, then be up front and say, "May I put you on hold just a moment? I am the only person here right now." Don't put someone on hold more than once. Otherwise you will stretch the boundaries of their patience and the elasticity of their goodwill. There is a certain amount of inference that the unknown caller is more important than they are.

R. If you have your calls screened so that a caller has been announced to you, recognize the caller immediately with, "David, this is Margarita. Good morning." Don't pick up the phone with, "Margarita Porto, here." It is an impersonal way to greet someone when you are supposed to know their name.

S. If your calls go through a receptionist first but aren't screened, answer your phone, "David Deans, here," or "Good morning, this is David Deans." If you are answering the phone at someone else's desk, answer with, "This is Janis Allen's desk."

T. Return all calls within twenty-four hours or have someone at your office follow up.

U. If you call someone and are disconnected, you are responsible for redialing, even if they accidently hung up. Since you placed the call, you know how to reach them.

V. If someone walks into your office while you are on the phone, motion them out the door or into a seat, but don't interrupt your phone conversation.

W. If you put someone on speaker phone, be certain to tell them immediately. "Larry, I have Sheri Underwood and Joey Clifton with me." Sheri and Joey should then greet Larry.

X. When you mistakenly take a phone call that you are not prepared for, spend a few minutes on the phone as a courtesy and then reschedule it at a later date. You will lose presence when you aren't prepared.

Y. If a client or co-worker is, for legitimate reasons, extremely angry on the phone, quietly listen without interjecting anything. Then, using tact, state your case. If you end up going in circles, suggest you need more information and then set up a phone meeting. If anger disintegrates into rudeness or abusiveness, don't respond. Just calmly say, "I will call you back tomorrow." End of conversation.

Z. Even if you are in a rush, say good-bye, but then wait for it to be reciprocated. Otherwise, it feels like you have hung up on them.

MOBILE PHONES, AIRLINE PHONES

Three years ago I was driving down Interstate 75 in Atlanta and my new mobile phone rang. I picked it up and was surprised to hear a voice I didn't recognize. The caller was the chairperson of a major convention in Seattle and their keynote speaker, Marlo Thomas, had just been in a minor car accident, and the convention needed to book another speaker within the next thirty minutes for the following day. They were asking me to replace her.

From her car phone, the chairperson had called my partner in his car. My partner then gave her my mobile number.

The bottom line was that not only did our car phones link us up within seconds, they also afforded my company a certain presence that allowed us to close the deal in ten minutes. We weren't able to send a copy of my book, a press kit, or testimonial letters, but the excitement of being able to hook up quickly and make things happen created a momentum that resulted in an important speaking engagement.

What kind of image do car or mobile phones create? That as a professional:

- your time is . . . valuable;
- your product is . . . important;
- your client's need is . . . urgent.

Mobile phones are not toys for the wealthy anymore. They are an ever-growing tool that offers not only convenience and immediacy but also a measure of presence.

Telephones in commercial airplanes are extremely convenient for urgent business. The biggest drawback is the expense. Always identify to the caller that you are on an airline phone to afford your conversation the urgency and importance it deserves.

THE NEXT BEST THING TO BEING THERE

Utilizing the latest and most effective high-tech methods of communicating will enhance your power and capability. Your electronic presence is part of your professional presence. It affords the best method to create a powerful impact when you can't be there in person.

Part III

---◆---

PLAYING OFFICE POLITICS: THE HAZARD ZONE

CHAPTER SEVEN

OFFICE GRAPEVINE VERSUS OFFICE GOSSIP

An important customer just gave you a week at his condo on the beach in gratitude for a recent job well done. Or, the client who has been your greatest source of income just declared bankruptcy. What's the first thing you want to do in either case? Tell someone, of course!

Celebrating, or commiserating, with office staff or colleagues helps us gain perspective on both triumphs and disasters. Talking things over with others helps to humanize the work and the workplace. One of the biggest reasons that offices located in the home fail is simply because there is no one to talk to. Not being able to share exciting news, or get a pep talk when things are going badly, is a distinct disadvantage.

On the other hand, companies point to idle chatter and water cooler gossip as the worst offenders that contribute to unproductive time. Vicious gossip has often been the cause of ruined careers, and whole companies have deteriorated because of unfounded industry rumors. Both McDonald's and Procter & Gamble have been detrimentally affected by several totally unfounded but widely circulated national rumors. In fact, it took Procter & Gamble ten years to finally win a judgment based on a "Satanic" rumor that was started by just one couple in Topeka, Kansas.

The couple had indicated to a number of their multi-level customers that the logo used by P & G represented a Satanic image. Actually it was a design that Procter & Gamble had created over a century ago and was not at all connected with the devil. Yet the rumor mill generated thousands of phone calls to Procter & Gamble by consumers who were concerned that their corporate profits were going to the devil.

HANDLING VICIOUS GOSSIP

When an employee begins to lose power within the ranks, or starts to lose face with co-workers and customers, maintaining professional presence becomes critical. If you find yourself in that uncomfortable position, don't act too hastily.

Don't curtail your activities and new projects just because of criticism or gossip. Cool off, calm down, think it through and devise a clear strategy to get things back on track.

Find the person or persons who are the source of the unfounded information. Calmly confront the source of a rumor to counteract and control the damage. Because the tendency is to walk away from a conflict, it is often very disarming to be directly confronted by someone that has been wronged. Often the "rumor source" immediately apologizes and stops the flow of dishonest information. Although gossip cannot be entirely eliminated, we can learn to control it.

The president of one of the local banks made the front page of the business section the same day he was to attend one of my seminars. In the one paragraph write-up, the reporter indicated that he was rumored to be fired. He called the reporter who wrote the article and asked where he got his information. The reporter told the president. Then my client, in his most calm and pleasant manner, called the informer and said, "The information in today's business section about my eminent demise from the bank has been traced to you. I wonder if you can tell me if it's true?"

The misinformed informant began to sputter, stammer, and then confess about "misspeaking concerning the bank president." He said he would call the newspaper with a corrected report that indicated the rumor wasn't true.

THE GRAPEVINE'S ACCURACY

When an organization is under stress, rumors abound and tempers run short. When unpopular decisions are made, gossip comes with the territory. In such an atmosphere, clear communication with people above and below you is especially important. With both, it's essential to stop rumors before they grow and get totally out of hand.

There is good news and bad news about the office grapevine. The bad news is that it is impossible to dismantle, discourage, or get rid of it. The good news is that this informal communications network is usually over 80% accurate.

So don't tune out; it's better to tune in. Listening to grapevine gossip can help a manager not only uncover poor attitudes and problems but also develop troubleshooting strategies. It's easier to maintain professional presence when you know what's going on behind the scenes.

Most active boards of directors, including major investors, will have "ears" in a company. They want to know what is really going on, not just what the officers report. How else can they learn about a personality who is causing conflict in the operation? That kind of thing is seldom written in a memo.

One company that I work with has a board of directors who are also investors in the firm. They attend staff meetings and regularly take lower level managers out to lunch, just to have regular chat sessions. Through grapevine information, they learn valuable data, which on a number of occasions was turned into sound decision making. When the directors learned that the office staff generally didn't need or desire elaborate, expensive office space but preferred regular salary increases, office expenses were substantially cut by moving out to the suburbs, and part of the monies saved was allocated to merit raises.

Other issues in the office can only be revealed through tuning into the grapevine. The employee's manual can't list the people who are best avoided. Get smart and listen in. The grapevine also can help you to understand where a company's priorities lie. Often what is claimed to be company policy and what actually happens are two different things.

THE "MOTHER MARY" SYNDROME

Most business people spend a third of their lives with their office family. They share confidences, victories, and insecurities. When you're new on the job, however, you need to be wary of the established employee who immediately latches on to you and tries to be the source of all information about everyone in the office. There may be a hidden agenda that will cause problems later.

In one Midwest manufacturing company there is a certain office manager who tries to manipulate all new hires. Everyone calls her "Mother Mary" because of the way she attaches herself to any new employee in a pseudo-nurturing manner.

She corners newcomers in the hallway or at the water cooler, establishing a premature level of confidence by sharing office gossip and her evaluations of other employees. Unfortunately, she so prejudices the new personnel in the office that they invariably start off on the wrong foot.

Part of the problem is that none of her co-workers respect her or want much to do with her. But she wants to be part of the office family, so she turns to the unsuspecting new employee who understandably wants to make friends and become established. One interesting development is that the other employees have begun to watch new hires and judge their ability to size up a bad situation by how quickly they unhook themselves from "Mother Mary." Whether you are a new employee or not, if you find yourself the recipient of too much gossip about others, remaining noncommittal and a bit unattached is the best option. You can diffuse the gossiper's effect with statements such as, "I really don't know Liz, so I'd like to form my own opinion about her." Or, "I've only met him briefly. He seems very capable."

Having power and presence means getting your own information from various sources before forming an opinion. Getting too cozy with someone you don't know and making judgments based on hearsay can be deadly to getting along with your office family as a whole.

When employees want to commiserate with you on their difficult boss, their untalented administrative staff, or their miniscule merit raise, play the role of a concerned cousin, not an overly sympathetic parent. Listen with concern, be a part of the office family, but don't entangle yourself by offering too much advice.

WHEN TOO MUCH IS REVEALED

Keeping personal secrets is difficult. Keeping professional secrets is even more difficult. However, since knowledge is power, it is a mistake to get loose-lipped and mention something to a colleague that can never be retracted. It is equally uncomfortable to know that someone has the "goods" on you.

Once private information has been passed on, it is no longer a secret. Research has determined that less than 1% of the population can keep a secret. Don't risk being the central topic of office gossip by sharing any information that could backfire.

If you have mistakenly shared too much personal information with the wrong individual, or let something slip by accident, do damage control. Sit down with them, request confidentiality concerning what you disclosed, but don't show obvious signs of panic. Most business people will show consideration and not repeat your secrets. The other, smaller percentage will repeat it, anyway. All you can do when the wrong people know your secrets is to forgive yourself and vow to be more careful in the future.

If you need to confess, seek out someone who is not connected professionally to you or your business and will remain loyal. Passing along information that could harm you years down the road is a calculated risk of letting down your hair and becoming friends with someone in business. Most of us do it. We need the intimacy of sharing concerns. We just need to be careful of whom we choose and what we divulge.

PERSONAL ISSUES TO AVOID WITH ALL CLIENTS AND MOST COLLEAGUES

- Details of a pending divorce
- Bankruptcies
- Illicit affairs
- Secrets known about bosses or coworkers
- Salary levels

PROFESSIONAL ISSUES TO AVOID WITH ALL CLIENTS, ALTHOUGH THIS INFORMATION MAY BE CAREFULLY SHARED WITH APPROPRIATE COMPANY COLLEAGUES

- Client confidences
- Customer complaints
- Closely held company information, like the actual cost of goods for a best-selling product
- Sales figures that are not public knowledge
- New products that have not yet been introduced. Many computer companies have regretted sharing this type of information with customers. If a product on the drawing board is smaller, better, and cheaper, then why would a customer buy the existing product?

James, a client of mine in Miami, told me that when a competitor confided that his company was having trouble with a new product, James was able to land a big order. He was amazed at how loose-lipped his competitor had been with highly confidential information.

During his next sales call with the buyer they both called on, James simply dropped a few hints about his competition's problems. The buyer decided not to hold back $50,000 of his budget waiting for a product that might never hit the market. James got the buyer to redirect his open-to-buy to James's company.

LET THE GRAPEVINE DO THE TALKING

If you get invited to the boss's house and others in the office weren't, don't mention your good fortune. This is not the same as self-promotion. Similarly, if you received an invitation to attend a holiday party at a client's home and others involved with the client didn't, avoid the urge to brag about it. If you begin to socialize with the boss, or the boss's boss, the word will get around, and the grapevine will be a much more powerful acknowledgment of your success.

KNOW WHEN TO HOLD 'EM, KNOW WHEN TO FOLD 'EM

One of the rules of corporate conversation is not to communicate everything that comes to your mind. If someone has been mysteriously let go, don't flame the flames with, "I am pretty sure that she was embezzling from the company. She always looked too well dressed for her salary."

These kinds of remarks are not only pure speculation, they are also professionally naive. If you can't clearly prove any public statement you make, you are contributing to gossip and discord. In business, you will never go wrong if you are generous with your praise and stingy in stating your own biases. Sometimes we need to hold our cards close to the chest and keep personal opinions to ourselves.

CHAPTER EIGHT

CONVERSATION IN THE OFFICE: DO'S AND DON'TS

Knowing what to say, when to say it, and to whom is an art. Having the ability to enjoy a lively discussion with the mailroom clerk and then switching gears for a black-tie event with your boss requires skill in the technique of good conversation.

The basis of good conversation is discovering what makes the other person feel accomplished. Add an animated expression and you will project that you are listening to someone who is smart, clever, and informed.

THE ART OF HEALTHY CONVERSATION

The weather is one topic that is presumed safe and therefore healthy for business. But even the safest of topics can be disastrous.

Meet Anthony Zone. He is a damage appraiser for an insurance company and usually works in the field. When he returns to the office on sunny spring days the secretaries make envious remarks about what a cushy job he has driving around in the sunshine while they're tied to their desks. He gets upset when they don't understand that his job entails fighting traffic, avoiding guard dogs in wrecking yards, and crawling around under cars rain or shine. For Anthony and his co-workers, the weather is not a safe topic.

If you live in St. Petersburg or San Jose, don't compare the cold, the wind, and the snow of Chicago to your hometown when you call on a client in the Windy City. An attendee at one of my seminars told me that he really put his foot into his mouth when he joked about Michigan's crummy, cold weather and Atlanta's 250 days of sunshine during a training session he did for a Detroit automobile company.

His Detroit colleagues were not amused. In fact, he spent the rest of his time there trying to make up for initially rubbing everyone in the class the wrong way.

Sports are usually an interesting topic of conversation, especially to men. Although a number of women don't avidly follow sports, the smart business woman will read at least the front page of the sports section to know which teams are playing. With just a few highlights, she will be able to either initiate or enter the conversation should it turn to athletics.

It simply isn't cute anymore for a woman to think that the Pirates are part of the National Football League or that the Oakland A's have a team of very tall basketball players. If a woman wants to appear savvy in business, she better know something about sports. Keeping up with a client's sports interest serves as a form of courtesy.

Cars can be an enticing topic. Automobiles are general enough, fairly noncontroversial, and most people own one. But don't bring up cars, just to talk about your new Jaguar.

Families and children are great as a topic, but only if clients or coworkers have children, too, or show a keen interest. Cute stories about one's children create boredom if your conversational partner lives in a singles' complex downtown, and plays racquetball for three hours every evening.

You can certainly ask co-workers or clients about their plans for the weekend. This will generally provide fertile ground for more conversation. At a banking cocktail hour one Thursday night, I was talking to the branch manager, who looked as though he might do a lot of hunting and fishing. I asked him what he was planning to do over the weekend. He said he was going to a Flamenco Dancer's Convention in Canada. We had a great time discussing his surprising avocation. Weekend activities can give you a window into an individual's personal life and create lively conversation without having to get too nosy.

My neighbor in Atlanta sleeps in the bed that Al Capone slept in. He describes it as a rather small little number with a great deal of lapis and gold gilding. He is also a collector of hundreds of other curiosities. Dropping a few little personal tidbits appropriately in conversation usually generates some interest in a business setting.

STAYING INFORMED

Current events are usually good topics. But if you're the one introducing them, stay neutral. Don't be too opinionated on any subject until you are certain your opinion will not antagonize clients or bosses.

Reading your daily newspaper, *USA TODAY* or *The Wall Street Journal*, gives an important update on world events. Watching a news program like "Headline News," CNN, or any of the morning shows, especially in their first hour of broadcasting, will make certain that you are not in the dark about vital, news-breaking issues.

For example, Frank, a friend of mine, mentioned to a client that he was on his way to San Francisco. He felt embarrassed when she said, "Gosh, I thought everyone knew. The big earthquake yesterday has closed the airports." Professionals who grasp what is happening in the world and are current on news events appear to be current in business too . . . right on top of things and generally knowledgeable. Business trends and reactions increasingly are a reflection of what is happening worldwide.

When the Berlin Wall first came down, the coverage was so thorough, the event so exciting, and the business opportunities so limitless that it astounded the entire table when a trainer at a major international corporation stopped the conversation with a, "Now, what's happened in Berlin?"

New television programs spark lively discussions. Even with busy lives, most people now videotape a favorite show to stay current. From prime-time TV to PBS to what's on HBO this week, television shows offer a medium that invites comment and safe, lively conversation.

The theater, symphony, ballet, and opera are rich topics, but only if your partner in conversation is an avid fan. Even if you know nothing about these things, being able to ask the right questions and listening intently is all that is required.

"Where did you go to school?" is not an inquiry about where you spent the first twelve years of your education. It is only an appropriate question if you are certain the person went to college, and if you haven't prejudiced yourself beforehand about any school. Some professionals will wear a college ring in business simply as a way to begin a conversation and thus cultivate a business relationship.

Current bestselling business books are always a good bet. So are movies. If you loved a movie, like *War of the Roses*, and your client hated it, don't lobby for your point of view unless it is done in exceedingly good humor. Restaurants, vacations, and leisure activities are also easy to discuss.

DANGEROUS CONVERSATIONS

When controversial topics like abortion, animal rights, or Japanese trade policies are introduced, it's best to stay neutral if you are with customers. Even if you have strong opinions, you can win the battle and lose the war should you belong to the opposite camp. If you find out with certainty that you are in the same camp with your customer, then you can carefully offer your viewpoint.

Avoid discussions of most medical issues. No one cares whether you have shin splints or sinus infections. Sharing the details of gall bladder surgery or a push-by-push account of a difficult labor is never good office or cocktail conversation.

Sexual conversation is usually a mistake. Discussing your vasectomy with a group of women could easily be misinterpreted. I attended a dinner with a conservative banker and six other business people when the banker pulled out a sex quiz that had appeared in that month's issue of *Playboy* magazine. She went around the table polling us about very intimate issues that embarrassed her guests. She thought it would lighten up the conversation because the quiz was tongue in cheek, but in her ill-conceived attempts to engage us, she alienated everyone.

Certainly both religion and politics are loaded and emotional topics. If you unexpectedly find yourself at odds with a client over any sensitive issues, quickly suggest "agreeing to disagree," and move the conversation onto safer ground. Ending with, "I certainly respect your position on that" helps maintain their respect for you.

Discussions about prices or the cost of things is tacky and classless. I overheard a conversation between a young accountant and a well-established restaurant owner, who was fretting over the maintenance cost of his Rolls-Royce. The young accountant limply interjected that the tune-up on her Toyota was $98 and that seemed like a lot of money.

Talking about your housekeeper, nanny, gardener, personal trainer, or your banker to someone who has no need of, desire for, or ability to pay for these particular services, is snobbish and rude. What is the point of clearly pointing out different socio-economic levels except to embarrass? Rarely is anyone of quality ever impressed.

Never discuss your income with anyone, except the IRS and your spouse. Net worth is no yardstick of real worth, despite what the arbitrageurs try to tell the world. Either you are making more money or less money than the person you are talking to. Where do you go from there except to start to compare "toys"?

NAME DROPPING

In most corporate and societal circles, name dropping is common and pervasive. It creates a potential connection and shows the kind of company that you keep. As business becomes more complex and diversified, it allows a kind of connecting between people who often don't know each other at all. It can create an entrance into a relationship that would otherwise not happen. It also provides an affiliation and can, at the very least, keep a conversation going.

The only safe way to drop names is authentically. When I worked for Bonne Bell Cosmetics, people would say they ran 10-K races with our company president, "Jesse" Bell, on a regular basis. I knew they hadn't even shared a cup of Gatorade. The reason was simple: No one ever called him "Jesse." He was always called Jess.

No one who knows Estée Lauder ever refers to her as Estée. She is always referred to as Mrs. Lauder. William Buckley's very social wife is known as Mrs. Buckles or Patsy in New York circles. But if someone says they know Patty Buckley, it is a sure give-away that they never met her.

It is more powerful to have your associations with others revealed discreetly through a longer relationship than sheer name dropping would permit. But business moves too quickly and relationships must be forged when the moment presents itself. So if you know a prominent business person, or have even attended the seminar of a well-known speaker and engaged in a five-minute conversation after the presentation, use the experience to your professional advantage.

CHAPTER NINE

THE OFFICE ROMANCE

Amanda and her boss, Bill, worked at the same management company. After two years of working together, Amanda invited Bill to her home for dinner. That began a very intense relationship that could have potentially destroyed their careers. But once they knew a strong relationship was inevitable, they mapped out a strategy to keep both romance and careers intact.

Bill told his boss exactly what was happening and secured his promise to keep it confidential. Bill and Amanda agreed that no letters, memos, fax transmittals, or intimate phone conversations would take place in the office. They also agreed not to pull any stunts like going into the stockroom together, locking the door and not emerging for forty-five minutes. Bill resolved to be a little more visibly demanding on Amanda at work, just to be certain that no one accused him of favoritism.

One year later they announced their impending marriage to the flabbergasted office staff. No one had suspected that Bill and Amanda even liked each other, since they seemed to be rather indifferent, and Bill definitely did not play favorites because he frequently gave Amanda the least desirable assignments.

LOVE IN THE OFFICE

Handling chemistry at the office is part of maintaining professionalism. An office romance is bound to happen at one time or another in every business person's career. Either it will happen to you or to someone in your company whom you know well. The issue is not that it happens but how well it is handled.

If we define ourselves by our work, as many of us do, then seeing the traits and characteristics in others that we value in ourselves can be a real turn-on. Self-confidence, intelligent decision making, poise, charisma, and adept people skills are alluring traits that can be a potent magnet in the workplace.

There is also a power aspect. Dating a superior or a superstar at the office has an allure. It is similar to a freshman dating a senior in high school. Sometimes it is almost a mentoring relationship, wherein the junior person learns firsthand from an executive. The junior person is exposed to positioned people, to exclusive locations, and high-powered situations where he or she normally would have no access.

Often, the excitement of being on a team and making things happen can be a powerful bond. When a large sale happens, the feeling of euphoria can stir up romantic feelings that might previously have been held in tight rein. Professional admiration can turn into something more.

IT'S NOT A MEAT MARKET

With the number of hours that most professionals devote to their careers, it is natural that we look for dates and potential spouses at work. Who has the time, energy, or ego to waste at the bar scene?

The reality is that romance at the office is as common as copier machines. More romances start in the office than in any other environment. Often people will interview at a particular company solely because it has the reputation for employing a high caliber of individual. Why not take advantage of a company's professional screening process to work alongside the best and the brightest? For someone new to a city, this may be the only safe place to find a date.

So the environment is ripe. There is not the awkwardness of a blind date. We get to know our co-workers on a multi-dimensional basis and we usually see them at their best. The office is a place where productivity counts, and professional goals are often the same.

HOW COMPANIES VIEW OFFICE ROMANCE

Generally the smaller the company, the more office romances are tolerated. The environment is more casual, and in general there are significantly fewer rules and procedures.

But the larger a company and the more established it is, the more it covertly or very overtly discourages romance between employees.

When a company does acknowledge the presence of romance, it

often does a poor job of handling it. Employees may be belittled, transferred against their will to other departments, or snidely made the butt of office gossip. In the worst-case scenario, especially when one partner is more expendable, a firing occurs.

If a company has a clear "no fraternizing" policy, both employees risk immediate dismissal with few questions asked. One large firm that I consult with has a clearly stated "no fraternizing" policy. When there are any known infractions, the respective bosses ask both parties into their office and give them one warning.

Then the parties involved are told to go home for three days to think about it, and if they agree with the company's decision, they still have a job. But if the relationship continues, they are swiftly given the sack. The only way to save their careers is if one employee volunteers to leave the company. The policy is clearly made known at the time of hiring and is expected to be unconditionally followed.

Because of the size, position, and confidentiality of the information that this company handles, this policy has merit according to the company officers. "We could be sued if any of our stockholders knew that a love affair was going on between our employees," one of the board members confided to me.

Most companies have found that this is a difficult policy to enforce fairly. They have also found that they have lost some of their best employees because of it. In one of my client's departments there was a significant "brain drain" because two experienced managers became involved with two salespeople, and the exit of four competent, well-trained, and romantically involved people left a gaping hole.

Also, if employees are forced to go elsewhere, they generally wind up at the competition, which is often a worse situation than having two amorous employees together in the same office.

Rather than make romance a part of the rules and regulations,

most companies tend to quietly discourage it. But when it does happen, they expect a certain level of professionalism to reign.

BIRDS AND BEES OF A VERY DIFFERENT FEATHER

There is a big difference, professionally, between an employee dating a married person and two single people having a mutually agreed upon tryst. Simply stated, it is nearly impossible to recover completely from a married affair. Once the word gets out about a married affair, it is a much more tantalizing bit of news than the two "new hires" heating it up at the company picnic.

Invariably, one of the employee's spouses will call, and unwitting office associates will spill the beans, or they will be in the awkward position of having to cover for the lovers. One of my clients told me about a husband who came bellowing into the office filled with employees and customers demanding that his unfaithful wife give him a divorce.

He had found out from her secretary that she had been in the Virgin Islands the previous week with her co-worker while she had told her husband that she had a sales meeting in Toledo. Although she had called home every day to allay suspicion, her husband decided to call the office to see where her paycheck was.

Our culture respects loyalty and devotion. We highly regard people who can make a commitment to their spouse and to their job. Because of our value system, there is always a suspicion in everyone's mind when a married affair is revealed. If this employee can be

so disloyal to someone they promised to be committed to, they are no doubt equally shallow and unfaithful to the company.

When an indiscretion of this magnitude is revealed, reputations are tarnished and professional stature, power, and presence are permanently damaged.

On the other hand, relationships between single people at most offices are generally acceptable if they are handled with discretion. And when the romance is over, it is very possible to completely recover from a single person's consenting relationship that went sour if both parties agree to a civilized parting.

KEEPING YOUR COOL WHEN YOU'RE HOT

All relationships require some ground rules. Office relationships require even more regulation and discretion because of the added dimension of bosses, co-workers, customers and income.

- At the onset of a relationship with a co-worker, don't confide in anyone who could blackmail you, unfairly discredit your work, or spread rumors. And don't make any announcements or even discuss your relationship with co-workers until you are clear on the level of mutual commitment. Wait until you are both well past the euphoria of the first date.
- Once your romance is common knowledge, be comfortable with it. Try to maintain the same attitude and demeanor as before. The more natural you are around your significant other, the more quickly others will accept the relationship.

- If you decide not to disclose your romance to anyone, don't try to cover up the affair by casting aspersions on the character of your lover. Remarks like, "He's always saying stupid things at the staff meeting," or, "She is such a nag about office procedure" will backfire.

- Don't send computer messages. They are rarely confidential and can be easily circulated around the office. One amorous employee at a manufacturing company had her torrid message intercepted and the prankster pushed two buttons and had it "delivered" to everyone with a computer terminal on their desk.

- Don't think you can make goo-goo eyes at your lover at the staff meeting and still maintain a professional reputation. Meaningful body language exchanges are as potent as words.

- Learn to be an actress or actor. You will be in many situations where you will have to convey feelings that don't exist and hide ones that do.

- Don't do anything that will generate jealousy from your loved one or from your staff. Flirting with a vendor in front of your significant other is an appalling mistake. Bragging about the instant tan you acquired at the sales convention in Barbados with your romantic associate will not endear you to the administrative staff.

- Love has the tendency to make us daydream and waste time. Create an environment that will make you stay focused. Consider working hours as completely off base for any romantic exchange. If nothing is communicated by memo, letters, flowers or interlude, then there will be minimal impact on your work and on others.

ALL YOU NEED IS LOVE ... AND
A BOSS WHO UNDERSTANDS

In some cases it is wise and in other cases it is dangerous to disclose your romance to your boss. A large part has to do with your performance on the job, your boss's temperament, and the prior precedent that has been set for inter-office relationships.

Here are the pros and cons of revealing your affair to your boss:

PROS

- You appear straightforward, honest, and professional.
- It may save your job down the line if the romance sours.
- If a co-worker brings it to the attention of your boss later, the issue will have already been discussed by the parties involved and the news won't take your boss by surprise.
- You have the chance to demonstrate how adept you are at handling difficult situations by making the boss aware of the romance, then handling it with great discretion.

CONS

- Your work may be more scrutinized and your boss may be more suspicious of requests for personal time off or an extended business trip.

- A longer lunch hour, late arrival in the morning, or an exit at 4:00 P.M. may cause misgivings, even if everyone else in the office does it.
- You may get transferred or moved to another position because your boss feels that your romance will put unnecessary stress on the rest of the staff.
- You may be fired.

ONCE AN AFFAIR IS OVER

The most difficult part of an office affair is the aftermath. It is hard enough getting over a love affair without having to face that person in the office every day or even every week at the staff meeting. Probably the most important reason co-workers decide not to pursue a relationship is because of the ramifications of a breakup and not because they don't see the potential for a good romance.

Here are four principles to maintain until the emotional part is over.

1. Don't immediately find someone else to date at the same office. You will appear extremely shallow and insecure, and it will seriously damage your professionalism.

2. After a breakup, there is a real sense of vulnerability, when you know that probably half the office will be gossiping about it. But don't break down in a show of emotion or cause a scene. Decide what you will need to maintain your sense of control and power, and then follow it. It may be a two-week vacation in the Caribbean to gain

perspective or evenings filled with night courses to complete your degree.

(3.) Consider a transfer to another department if you feel constantly vulnerable and unable to perform well. But don't take a demotion to do it.

(4.) Don't let petty jealousies get in the way of rebuilding a new relationship with the former lover. The ability to refrain from saying anything unkind about a past relationship is tremendously impressive to co-workers.

HANDLING AN AFFAIR WHEN YOU ARE NOT INVOLVED

A client of mine, Helen, told me that she was in a very difficult romantic dilemma several years ago. Her boss, Michael, was having an affair with two women at the same time who worked next to each other. At the end of the day, Michael would walk either into one woman's office or the other's for their evening together. He made it even more grim because he would never commit to either one which he would see that night.

Each woman would be certain to be back in her office by 5:00 P.M., even if it meant cutting an important meeting short, just to make sure she would be available. The tension between the two women who worked together and knowingly competed for this man made the office environment almost unbearable and the rest of the staff demoralized. There were daily outbursts of tears from one or the other, often over a matter that was directly related to this stressful affair.

My client realized that she had three choices: talk to Michael, talk to her co-workers Lee and Barb, or quit. She decided that the safest path was to discuss the situation with Lee, because she was closest to her. But Lee was so emotionally involved with Michael that Helen's advice went in one ear and out the other.

When she gingerly approached the subject with her boss, Michael, he became furious and defensive.

Helen felt that she had pursued every avenue of recourse and had given the situation almost a year to resolve itself. Her only other course was to go to the board members of the company, who had been longtime friends with Michael. She decided against approaching them.

So in desperation, she dusted off her resume, updated it, and found another job. Subsequently three other very bright people left the organization purely because of this mishandled, emotionally destructive, and very unprofessional office romance. It took several years before the department got back on track because of the talent drain.

WHAT'S LOVE GOT TO DO WITH IT?

Discussing someone's love affair at the office is infinitely more interesting than auditing last month's sales transactions. The higher up and the more visible in the organization the involved people are, the more they can count on being endlessly discussed by everyone below them.

Sometimes the press even gets involved, such as in the Bendix Corporation case where Mary Cunningham ended up leaving Bendix after intense pressure from the company and a constant spotlight from the newspapers. The situation at Calvin Klein several years ago with the principle of the company and an employee is another example of a personal romance that found its way into the front page, no doubt with distortions.

When a romance springs up at the office, the first rule is not to gossip about it. More than any other area, no one has firsthand knowledge about someone else's love affair.

Don't contribute anything even if you know what is going on. Also, by not gossiping, you won't get the reputation for being the source of all the sordid office information. Don't casually bring up the relation-ship with the involved persons, especially if they are senior to you. It is political suicide.

If you are sandwiched in between an affair (your boss is dating someone who works for you) and you feel squeezed, call a meeting with your boss and discuss the situation professionally. Don't say anything that will discredit your boss's good judgment. You may decide not even to bring up the romantic angle, just the fact that you are not able to do your job well because you are not getting the support from a specific staff member. A genuine sense of re-sentment will develop if your authority is being undermined by the affair, especially when it comes from someone who reports to you.

Never stoop to personal attacks, even if you feel they are justified. "She is such a fool. He will never leave his wife. And he is such a lecher, I don't know what she sees in him anyway, except for his money, of course." Throwing dirt will only cause you to lose ground. Also, if you appear to be noncommittal and nonjudgmental through-out the affair, you will win points from both parties and from the entire office staff, too.

Don't become the constant sounding board for one of the involved parties. When the affair is over, you will look very aligned to one party, and it could put you in an awkward position. Sometimes it is better not to have too much information.

THE CASE OF THE NEWLYWEDS

One of my clients told me that the most disruptive romance in her career was between two married people . . . who were married to each other! Her co-worker was so starry-eyed, so totally emotionally invested in her new husband that nothing got done in the office.

Between flower deliveries, balloon deliveries, intimate phone calls, lunch and dinner reservations, and a regular polling of the office staff on the best vacation spots, the entire day seemed to be devoted to love.

Everyone agreed that a secret, torrid affair would have been much more amenable to the office staff, because then some work would get done. With everything so public, with long, passionate kisses twice a day in the reception area in front of clients, everyone wished they would just knock it off and get back to business.

Finally the woman's boss simply sat her down and told her that although everyone wished her happiness in her marriage, all the time that was being taken away from business was demoralizing to her co-workers and staff. She apologized and shaped up.

DON'T THROW BOUQUETS AT ME

The healthiest way to have an affair with a co-worker is to first determine if the affair is serious and worthy of a major commitment.

If it's not, then the risk is probably too great. A mere dalliance in love may prove too complicating for the office.

If the relationship is worth continuing, these are the easiest romances to maintain:

- Single
- Consenting
- Heterosexual
- Similar levels but different departments

Departing from any one of these four characteristics will not necessarily doom a relationship. But it is certain to cause more headaches and heartaches.

Part IV

◆

THE
COMFORT ZONE:
PUTTING YOURSELF
AND OTHERS
AT EASE

CHAPTER TEN

THE IMPACT OF A BUSINESS WARDROBE

Although time marches on and trends and influences directly affect our choices in business clothing, three things haven't changed.

1. If you want the job, you have to look the part.
2. If you want the promotion, you have to look promotable.
3. If you want respect, you have to dress as well as or better than your industry standards.

WELL-SUITED FOR BUSINESS

Let's start with the most expensive investment . . . suits. They require more of a capital outlay than any other piece of clothing. The increased cost of fabric is the primary reason that the price of suits has skyrocketed. Fabric accounts for approximately two-thirds of the price of a garment today.

Few women or men have the resources for assembling scores of expensive business suits. But many of us have been brainwashed to strive for variety in appearance so that we purchase inexpensive, trendy fashions simply to have a different look every day. This technique is a proven disaster, both financially and in terms of job advancement. Purchasing quality, not quantity, is solid advice.

A wardrobe plan will maximize your clothing dollar if you stick to it. Know exactly what your next five purchases need to be. There is so much inventory in so many stores that unless you are armed with a clear plan, you could easily end up with just more stuff cluttering up the closet.

The good news about a wise suit purchase is that the suit can be worn until it literally wears out. Men who purchase classically can feel comfortable investing their money knowing that the styling details of a quality suit were established years ago and have withstood the test of time. Although women can't always count on the same timeline for their major pieces, they *can* count on the fact that good fabric, appropriate colors, and fine styling will compliment them and camouflage their weak spots.

Every industry has its own requirements. Let's look at four categories of business and the appropriate images for each one included on pages 143-150. All the charts in this chapter will refer back to these four representative categories.

THE CATEGORY: *Traditional*

THE REPRESENTATIVE BUSINESSES

Firms and businesses that are fiscal and traditional in orientation: banks, insurance firms, legal and accounting firms, stock brokerage firms, large computer firms, government, and companies that have been in business more than 50 years

Long hair and an ill-fitting suit will damage the image of even the most accomplished professional. She needs a better fit, shorter hair, makeup, and toned hosiery.

Before

A smooth bob, well-applied makeup, and larger earrings accent her face. Her suit is updated, but still conservative. Her toned hosiery and black pumps complete her polished appearance.

After

Before

A three-piece suit in a light color with dated styling is not professional. In traditional businesses, beige should be worn sparingly. The flap pockets and flared trousers are not appropriate. The sunglasses should be inside the breast pocket.

After

A two-piece wool suit in a medium-weight fabric in navy blue is the ultimate corporate look. A crisp, long-sleeve white shirt, a silk tie with a red background, and a leather briefcase add polish to this powerful look.

THE CATEGORY: *Contemporary*

THE REPRESENTATIVE BUSINESSES

Growth firms that are very sales and marketing oriented: small to medium size computer companies, advertising agencies, pharmaceutical companies, real estate firms, telephone and communications companies, upscale automobile dealerships

A constructed, man-tailored business suit is tired-looking. The A-line skirt, Peter Pan collar, and small ribbon add to an uninteresting look. Her hair needs a better cut and her glasses should not be tinted.

Before

An unconstructed jacket is flattering, updated and very useful over a variety of skirts. The padded shoulders, push-up sleeves, and rolled collar are elegant. Her haircut frames her face. Blended makeup and larger earrings add style.

After

Before

A stiff fabric is ungraceful and hangs like cardboard. Even in a darker color, a three-piece suit is dated. The striped tie needs to be replaced, too.

After

A rich wool medium-blue pinstripe with a pale pink shirt and paisley tie is updated and elegant. The skin belt adds luxury to the suit. Pleats on suit trousers have become a classic detail.

THE CATEGORY: *Bridge*

THE REPRESENTATIVE BUSINESSES

Businesses that require bridging both manual and office activity: engineering companies or departments, heavy manufacturing, and transportation

Two-piece dresses are appropriate, but only in the right fabric, style, and color. This sleeveless top is too tight. Her split skirt is too casual. Her hair needs a different shape, and she needs the refinement of makeup and better jewelry.

Before

A two-piece knit dress is slimming, wrinkle-free, and will look current for many years. Her hair has height, but is smooth on the sides, and her makeup accents her eyes. Her shined shoes finish this smart look.

After

Before

Short-sleeve shirts are not acceptable in any climate or any professional business. His hair needs styling, and his glasses need to be replaced with more current frames or contact lenses.

After

Styled hair with a dark two-piece suit and crisp shirt show a great deal of presence. His pocket square is pressed white linen, which matches the shirt, not the tie.

THE CATEGORY: *Fashion Forward*

THE REPRESENTATIVE BUSINESSES

Businesses with a creative orientation: retail, residential decorating, cosmetic companies, publishing, design firms, and creative businesses

Her long hair, long pearls, and long hemline drag down and shorten her silhouette. Even an expensive garment can't overcome a poor fit.

Before

A wool crepe two-piece suit with sophisticated Chanel piping is elegant, yet businesslike. With her hair done in a French knot, subtley applied makeup, and a strand of pearls, she presents a refined appearance.

After

A tight, European-cut jacket is not flattering or professional. His facial hair detracts from his appearance, and his trousers are cuffed too short.

Before

Clean-shaven with a well-trimmed moustache, his smile is more apparent. His jacket is a better color, fabric, and fit. The white pocket square adds a distinctive detail.

After

MEN'S STYLING

	TRADITIONAL	CONTEMPORARY	BRIDGE	FASHION FORWARD
Single breasted 2-button close	√	√	√	√
Single breasted 3-button close				√
Double breasted		√		√
Blazer Solid color			√	√
Jacket Patterned			√	√
Pleated suit trousers	√	√	√	√
Cuffed trousers	√	√	√	√
Uncuffed trousers	√	√	√	√

WOMEN'S SUIT STYLING

	TRADITIONAL	CONTEMPORARY	BRIDGE	FASHION FORWARD
Notched lapel	√	√	√	√
Collarless lapel	√	√		√
Double breasted	√	√	√	√

	TRADITIONAL	CONTEMPORARY	BRIDGE	FASHION FORWARD
Single breasted	√	√	√	√
Highly constructed (man-tailored)	√		√	
Unconstructed (push-up sleeves)		√		√
Slim skirt	√	√	√	√
Long pleated skirt	√	√	√	
Full, circle skirt				√
Above the knee skirt				√
Traditional hemline	√	√	√	

A FEW UPDATES ON MEN'S SUITS

Pleats on trousers have progressed from a very trendy look in the eighties to a business staple in the nineties. Most men's suits come with pleated trousers. Pleats provide interesting detail and allow more room and comfort.

Cuffed trousers have also made a comeback, and can set off a pair of tasseled business slip-ons beautifully. Shorter, heavier men should generally avoid cuffs. Very active men who rush around the office complain that their cuffs often get caught on their desk chair, or that they collect lint and dust in them. Although it is still a matter of body proportion and individual choice as to whether to cuff or not, most men who purchase pleated trousers do cuff. Either way, the trouser should be hemmed so that there is a slight break in the front.

The classic double-breasted suit can be very sharp, but there is always the nagging concern about its longevity and appearance. I advise my clients to purchase one only if the garment and the industry are right and they can answer yes to all four questions.

1. Do you look well in seven extra layers of fabric over your middle section—in other words, *are you thin enough?*
2. Is the button spacing appropriate for your height?
   A two-button spacing is better for a shorter man.
   A taller man can wear a four-button configuration.
3. Do other men in your industry wear double-breasted suits?
4. Have you already built a solid basic wardrobe of single-breasted suits?

SKIRT LENGTH: TOO SHORT CAN BE DANGEROUS

One of the most frequently asked questions from my seminar attendees, both male and female, is: "What is the correct skirt length for business?" The simple answer is: "Whatever is the most flattering to both your leg and your profession."

Consider what happens when you sit down in a short skirt. The skirt rises another four to five inches. Will you feel comfortable with your thighs showing?

Consider, too, the shapeliness of your legs. Actually, the shape of one's leg has more to do with heredity than anything else. But it would seem that no bright businesswoman would go out of her way to clearly expose something that is not an asset.

Then there is the issue of practicality. Most suits, separates, and dresses have a proportion to them that won't work if they are greatly altered. Hacking off seven inches from a skirt usually ruins the line and the silhouette. It will not update the look. If you are in a business that permits short skirts, get an expert tailor's advice before shortening your existing suit skirts.

Economically speaking, maintaining a consistent, personal standard for skirt length will save seasonal hassles and your wardrobe budget. The fashion standard since 1970 has reflected the following guidelines, which should help you determine the skirt length that's right for you.

- The most attractive place to end your hemline is at the thinnest part of the leg—usually where your calf curves into the knee.
- Stand in front of a three-way mirror. Try on skirts of various lengths, and then determine what your personal hemline should be for each style of skirt—slim, pleated, and full.
- Slim skirts look best just barely covering the knee, while pleated and full skirts should be considerably longer.

MEN'S SUITS: COLOR AND PATTERN

Men's suits generally get their interest from the pattern, like a pinstripe, windowpane, herringbone, or a tweed, and not from unusual color or styling. The following is a color and pattern chart for men's suits.

	TRADITIONAL	CONTEMPORARY	BRIDGE	FASHION FORWARD
Charcoal	√	√	√	√
Medium Gray	√	√	√	√
Navy Blue	√	√	√	√
Medium Blue	√	√	√	√
Khaki/Tan	√	√		√
Olive Green	√	√		√
Brown			√	
Taupe		√		√
Solid	√	√	√	√
White pinstripe	√			
Multi-colored pinstripe	√	√	√	√
Muted windowpane		√		√
Herringbone		√	√	√
Tweed/Textured	√	√	√	√

WOMEN'S SUITS: COLOR

Women's suits gain their interest from unusual color and styling, not generally the pattern.

	TRADITIONAL	CONTEMPORARY	BRIDGE	FASHION FORWARD
Black	√	√	√	√
Brown	√	√	√	√
Gray/Marble	√	√	√	√
Winter White		√		√
Taupe/Clay	√	√		√
Hunter Green	√	√	√	√
Emerald Green				√
Lime Green				√
Navy Blue	√	√	√	√
Turquoise	√	√	√	√
Cobalt Blue	√	√	√	√
Electric Blue		√		√
Pale Blue				√
Teal		√		√
Fuchsia				√
Rose				√
Red		√		√
Peach		√		√

	TRADITIONAL	CONTEMPORARY	BRIDGE	FASHION FORWARD
Purple/ Amethyst	√	√		√
Cranberry	√	√	√	√
Gold				√
Yellow				√
Olive	√	√	√	√

MEN'S SUITS: FABRIC

	TRADITIONAL	CONTEMPORARY	BRIDGE	FASHION FORWARD
Wool—medium weight	√	√	√	√
Wool—light weight	√	√		√
Poly-Wool		√	√	
Silk/Wool		√		√
Poplin	√	√		√

WHY SPEND MONEY ON A MORE EXPENSIVE WOOL?

Finer, more expensive wool has longer and softer threads. This means less itching and a more beautiful drape. It also means fewer wrinkles. Often a person who has an allergy to coarse wools can comfortably wear finer ones.

WOMEN'S SUITS: FABRIC

	TRADITIONAL	CONTEMPORARY	BRIDGE	FASHION FORWARD
Wool—gabardine	√	√	√	
Wool—crepe	√	√		√
Wool—light weight	√	√	√	√
Silk	√	√		√
Silk/Wool	√	√		√
Rayon		√	√	√
Cotton/Poly		√	√	√
Manmade or Blends		√	√	√

DRESSES: COLOR AND FABRIC

Dresses are an alternative look for business. Although they don't have the same amount of power and authority that a suit does, they are more comfortable and often more feminine. The two classic shapes are the *chemise*, which generally falls straight from the shoulders with a little shaping at the waist, and the *coat dress*, which buttons up the front. The following is a color and fabric chart for dresses.

	TRADITIONAL	CONTEMPORARY	BRIDGE	FASHION FORWARD
Black	√	√	√	√
Gray/Marble	√	√	√	√
Winter White		√		√
Taupe/Clay	√	√		√
Hunter Green	√	√	√	√
Emerald Green		√		√
Navy Blue	√	√	√	√
Cobalt Blue	√	√	√	√
Teal		√		√
Fuchsia				√
Red		√		√
Purple/ Amethyst	√	√		√
Cranberry	√	√	√	√
Olive	√	√	√	√
Wool	√	√	√	√
Silk	√	√		√
Rayon	√	√	√	√
Manmade or Blends	√	√	√	√

MEN'S SHIRTS

The best fabric is 100% cotton, nicely starched in long sleeve, with approximately ½ inch of shirt linen showing under the jacket sleeve.

	TRADITIONAL	CONTEMPORARY	BRIDGE	FASHION FORWARD
White	√	√	√	√
Pale Blue	√	√	√	√
Pale Pink	√	√		√
Red Striped	√	√	√	√
Blue Striped	√	√	√	√
Buttoned-down		√	√	√
Straight Collar	√	√		√
French Cuff	√	√		√
Monogram	√	√		√

THE SHIRT ON YOUR BACK

Three new practices concerning shirts have recently become the norm for those with professional presence. The first is that nearly all businessmen get their shirts commercially laundered. The crisp look is very important in business nowadays, and few people have the time or the expertise to create that effect without help.

The second change is that French cuffs are readily available in off-the-rack shirts. For many years the only way to purchase French cuffs was to order a custom shirt. Now, all department stores and men's clothing stores stock the French cuff.

The third is the predominance of custom shirts. Many men want the most flattering shirt for their bodies and they can't always find it off-the-rack. Most men have a difficult time finding a label that has the right sleeve length, collar spread, fabric content, color, plus a long enough shirttail. They may also prefer not to have a pocket, especially if much of their present shirt wardrobe has been ruined because of ink stains.

Although custom shirts cost a little more, need to be ordered in groups of four, and often take a month to ship, most of my clients love them. They are offered in a wide selection of colors and fabrics including conservative pinpoint oxford or beautiful Egyptian cotton.

WOMEN'S BLOUSES

This is a color chart for women's business blouses.

	TRADITIONAL	CONTEMPORARY	BRIDGE	FASHION FORWARD
White/Cream	√	√	√	√
Fuchsia	√	√		√
Purple	√	√	√	√
Pink	√	√	√	√
Jade	√	√	√	√
Turquoise	√	√	√	√
Paprika		√		√
Silk	√	√		√
Rayon	√	√		√
Quality Manmade	√	√	√	√
Cotton	√	√	√	√

ADDING QUALITY TO YOUR BLOUSE COLLECTION

Many women have about thirty blouses and wear only five or six of them on a regular basis. When I question my seminar clients, they indicate that the blouses they love to wear are the ones that they spent the most money on.

A beautiful, excellent-quality blouse will dress up a suit like nothing else. Although silk is generally a wonderful fabric for blouses, it comes in different qualities and weights. The best choice is a heavier weight silk, which almost always means it is of good quality. Manmade fabric can closely resemble silk and is a more economical choice because it can be laundered at home.

Rayon is a popular fabric for blouses. It has the luxurious properties of heavy silk, is less expensive to purchase than silk, but still requires dry cleaning.

The surplice neckline has a beautiful crisscross drape in the front and is an excellent way to update a suit. The only risk is that it must have enough fabric in front to stay draped and not gape open. Pleating in the front and back is also elegant. In addition to the surplice, the easiest style to work with is the jewel neckline because it is easy to accessorize with jewelry and scarfs.

TIE TALK

The item that wastes the greatest amount of a man's clothing dollar hangs on his tie rack. Most men in my seminars own about thirty-five ties. The Tie Rack, a national chain of stores, indicates that 22.3 ties per American male is the average. The surprising part is that most men wear only five or six ties regularly. Generally the ties that are actually worn are of better construction in 100% silk. They also come in great colors.

Silk is still the best fabric for ties because it provides a wonderful contrast in texture when worn with a crisp, starched shirt. Silk also knots more securely. Even with the improvement in manmade fibers over the years, nothing will work better as a tie fabric than silk.

Today's look is more toward patterned ties rather than stripes or solids. Although most sports announcers still wear striped ties, the rest of the world is wearing foulards, prints, and patterns. The most avant-garde looks are those with an irregular, geometric, rather bold pattern. A more conservative look is the foulard, which is a small, intricate geometric pattern evenly spaced throughout the tie. Paisley print ties are a rich-looking choice.

BEST TIE COLORS: BOTH TRADITIONAL CHOICES AND MORE CONTEMPORARY

- Red in all shades
- Dark blue
- Teal
- Purple
- Mauve
- Olive
- Taupe

In terms of length, ties are being worn a little longer today. Since a more expensive tie is slightly longer, the acceptable length is between the middle and the bottom of the belt buckle.

One of the main complaints that I hear about ties is that they don't dry-clean well. As a matter of fact, many men simply throw a tie away once it has a grease spot. There are, however, several less drastic solutions. One is to find a dry cleaner that specializes in tie cleaning. The cleaning should be hand done, the edges should stay rolled, and the process will be expensive. The other solution is to purchase a high-quality fabric protector and spray all ties once, prior to wearing them. Although most fabric protectors are very safe on silk, be sure to test an inconspicuous part of the tie first. Also try it on just one tie to make sure that you are pleased with the way the tie knots. Fabric protectors add a very thin layer of residue and may slightly affect the way the tie is knotted.

DISTINCTIVE ACCESSORIES FOR MEN

- Crocodile or alligator belt—makes a suit look $100 more expensive
- Braces—not the clip-on variety, but in silk with leather attachments
- Starched linen pocket handkerchiefs—no silk for daytime
- Small cuff links—the most updated looks are gold or silver bars or balls, matte stones such as onyx or lapis, and rectangular or square shapes.
- An elegant watch—well worth the investment
- Thinner-soled shoes—more elegant

BRACES, BUT NOT THE DENTAL TYPE

Braces serve the same function as the often misnamed suspenders—only braces do it with more panache than clip-on suspenders. Braces are generally constructed of silk with leather attachments. They button onto trouser buttons. Several of my flight-attendant friends swear they can tell if a passenger is ticketed for first class or coach by how he wears his braces. If the braces are accompanied by a belt, he is definitely headed for coach. If the braces are expensive-looking, and the only thing holding up the trouser, that man will sit in first class.

UNISEX JEWELRY

"What about an earring for men?" I am often asked. "Aren't they permitted now for business? You see them everywhere."

Earrings are great . . . on women and on entertainers. But the message sent to corporate America by a man wearing an earring is a confusing one. Several male clients of mine in real estate decided to get one ear pierced but then only wear an earring on the weekends. The problem is that the holes are still very visible and create nearly the same image as if they were actually wearing an earring. Men's earrings and business are like oil and water: They don't mix.

ACCESSORIZING FOR WOMEN

A profusion of scarfs, belts, and jewelry clutters every woman's wardrobe. We overbuy, we neglect to wear, and we become overwhelmed by all these items. They provide the necessary flair and individuality we crave, but they are also confusing. The key to wearing accessories is to create a good system of organization in the closet using ready-made organizers or creating your own.

Most business women love large silk scarfs but seldom wear them. Gone is the small floppy tie; it's a dinosaur today. The last decade heralded in the beautiful designer scarf worn on the shoulder. But how in the world do you get anything done when it requires constant adjustment? The best scarf is the one that stays in place when tied and actually contributes to the pulling together of an outfit. It should not clutter or overwhelm. The most useful shape is oblong because it can be wrapped in many different ways, including the ascot.

To keep scarfs in order, purchase plastic clothes pins and clip four or five on a hanger. Then attach one scarf per pin. Household stores also sell inexpensive scarf hangers with clips. Chances are you will wear scarfs much more when they are hanging in the closet with your suits, blouses, and skirts instead of being folded and stored away in a drawer.

Classic skin belts with designer belt buckles can create an individual signature. More women are opting to take off their jackets at work, and a belt will give a finished look to a skirt and blouse. Reptile skin combined with suede or leather is texturally interesting and professionally elegant as long as the belt is not too large.

Costume earrings predominate, although gold earrings are always coveted. The problem with wearing gold is the potential of losing them. If you purchase gold earrings, insist on pierced with screw-on backs. Whether you select gold or costume earrings, constant telephone use loosens the clip or other attachment. More than one earring has landed silently on the carpet, been run over and flattened. Many woman select clip-on, costume pieces for comfort and convenience (rather than pierced). Larger pieces are best since tiny earrings get lost in a business look. Double-pierced ears or ear cuffs are not an appropriate corporate look.

Lapel pins in both modern and antique designs give flavor to a suit. The expensive Picasso scribble pin is very popular. It comes in sterling silver, or in solid gold with or without stones. It is being worn almost like a prized medal on a military jacket, a way to show achievement.

A gold watch is a treasure. So are real pearls. However, depending on your budget, there are certainly hundreds of good imitations for business. Daytime diamonds, especially champagne-colored ones, are very popular in rings, bracelets, and earrings as long as they aren't more than one carat.

DISTINGUISHED ADDITIONS FOR MEN AND WOMEN

1. Eyeglasses, particularly well-chosen tortoise shell frames, create an intense, intelligent look. Studies have indicated that you are perceived as being richer and smarter in glasses. In fact, "planos" are what those with perfect eyesight are wearing . . . clear glass in wonderful frames. Generally the frame should follow the line of the eyebrow and not extend too far on the side of the face.

2. Gold fountain pens have caught people's fancy. Antique pens, modern Mont Blanc, Waterman, and Parker fountain pens are very prestigious—like owning a Rolls-Royce—but much less expensive to purchase and less trouble to maintain.

3. An expensive-looking, leather briefcase is an excellent accessory purchase. Soft-sided and satchel types are the most current-looking.

GROOMING GUIDELINES

Shorter hair is an important part of a more updated look for both men and women. Toupees are out, wigs are gone, and whatever the amount of hair on the head, it needs to be shampooed regularly. Estimates are that 20% of men and 80% of women now color their hair to either cover the gray or to add highlights.

Beards have vanished and moustaches are on the wane. The advances in shaving products and razors mean that most men don't need to suffer from razor burn. Although men today are using less fragrance, they are using more skin-care products. Rough, chapped skin is not masculine.

Makeup is lighter and more neutral. The deep-bronzed tan for both men and women is fading from the corporate scene. Coco Channel came back from a cruise in the 1920s with a tan and instantly made it a status symbol for decades, but today it looks increasingly unattractive. This is an interesting change for the eye, because we have so long associated a deep tan with being rich and leisurely. Since a tan carries the threat of skin cancer and the certainty of wrinkles, it is no longer worth the risk.

Business professionals need to have hands that are extremely clean and well-groomed. Hands are constantly seen—when brochures are offered, products are shown, and contracts signed. Regular manicures, done either professionally or at home, are important. Gender does not play a role in well cared for hands. Nails for both men and women should be fairly short with cuticles pushed back.

Long, acrylic nails look dated on business women. Clear or subtly colored polish on nails that are ¼ inch beyond the fingertip is the most attractive look.

FOOTNOTES

While a lot of wasted dollars are devoted to men's ties and women's blouses, shoes are the other area of genuine waste. What most men and women today find is that they wear the same three pairs of shoes over and over again, black and brown for men; black, taupe, and navy for women. All leather is the most comfortable, and speaking about comfort, there is a revolution in women's footwear. Finally, manufacturers are producing good-looking leather pumps that are made to emulate a sneaker on the inside and they are reaching a very receptive group of foot-weary business women.

Pumps are the best-selling business shoe for women because they are the most flattering. If they are well-cut, they make the ankle and calf look slimmer and shapelier. They should not be more than 2½ inches in height.

Tasseled slip-ons are the best-selling business shoe for men because of the convenience and versatility factor. Wingtips still survive in colder climates, but only in very conservative industries.

TEETH AT THEIR BEST

One of the strongest personal business assets we can have is attractive teeth. They project a sense of good breeding and excellent health. For most, this doesn't happen naturally. Yellowed or brown teeth look unappealing, and crooked or chipped teeth are not aesthetically pleasing. Most people who don't like their teeth simply won't show them. The natural outcome is that they don't smile much and are branded unfriendly.

Teeth, however, can be capped, bonded, crowned, straightened, bleached, or shaped to look completely natural and attractive. All the mercury fillings can be removed and replaced with white composite that is the natural color of teeth. Aesthetic dentistry is one of the finest investments a business person can make.

IT MATTERS

Wardrobe . . . accessories . . . grooming: they are each an important part of the impression we create and how others continue to view us. No other business skill is as visible as the way we package ourselves. Image puts a frame around all our other, less visible business credentials.

CHAPTER ELEVEN

CRITICAL CIRCUMSTANCES AND STICKY SITUATIONS

Embarrassing moments that happen in the course of a workday compromise our sense of control and our sense of self. When we have looked ridiculous, the very thought of those occasions can still make us cringe, even months or years later. Embarrassment will often cause us to avoid important contacts, clients, or associates because they were present when we made a particular faux pas. However, when we react to an embarrassing situation with true professional presence we not only can avoid further damage to our image, we may actually enhance it.

Helen Neetle is one of my seminar attendees who told me an extraordinary story about her stickiest business situation. She was new in her city and new in her job as the office manager and supervisor for a growing firm—a job that promised an opportunity for future advancement. A member of a military family, she prided herself on being very organized and capable, arriving at work before 7:30 A.M. and often staying late.

As office manager, she made certain that no one except employees and clients parked in the company parking lot, because the firm's downtown location was inviting to freeloaders who wanted to avoid paying for parking. Normally, she relied on a lot attendant, but this particular Friday he was out sick.

Ever conscientious, Helen spent part of that day patrolling the lot. She immediately noticed a late-model Mercedes that she was certain didn't belong to anyone who worked in the building, nor was it registered as a client's car. After her second pass through the lot, she called the towing company and had the car removed. Thirty minutes after the tow truck pulled away from the building with the car, an irate man stormed into the reception area asserting that his car had been stolen. "Oh, no," the receptionist replied. "It was towed from our lot less than an hour ago."

Two minutes later, Helen, summoned by her boss, confidently swept into his office, only to find the CEO in a rage along with a man in a confused frenzy. They demanded an explanation about the towed vehicle. Helen was quickly made aware that the automobile she had had towed belonged to the company's most important client, who had been in an extended meeting off-site with Helen's boss.

Stunned, Helen turned scarlet and began to hyperventilate. Her body language changed from her usual large, sweeping, open gestures to closed, tiny movements, and she averted eye contact. She drew her arms and head into her body like a turtle defending itself and clung to the nearest door. Without an apology to the hapless client, she mumbled something about checking on the situation and went straight to her office where she called the receptionist with instructions on how the client could retrieve his car. Then she hung up the telephone, grabbed her purse, and fled through the back exit.

Why this sudden metamorphosis from a confident, self-assured woman to a cringing coward? Because nothing saps our self-confidence, impacts our body language, or stymies our effectiveness quite like being the brunt of a humiliating experience.

Helen made a bad situation worse when her embarrassment made her inept. Not only did her verbal skills deteriorate, but her nonverbal communication said that she was totally unable to handle the consequences of her mistake.

Essentially she "said," through her presence, that she wished to shrink and disappear. She left her boss in the throes of a most unpleasant situation that he did not create, and she inconvenienced an innocent client.

FACING THE MUSIC

What should she have done? First of all, never try to defend the indefensible. Helen should have accepted full responsibility for the mistake, and she should have made sure that no one else was blamed or implicated.

She should have kept her presence calm and professional, showing she was still in control of this unfortunate occurrence. Strong, direct eye contact and sympathetic but not victimized gestures would have gained her a lot of points while demonstrating her skill in handling problems.

Nodding and keeping a pleasant expression, while staying calm and oriented to the customer's needs, create the best possible scenario. Maintaining a respectful distance of three to six feet shows an awareness of the other person's anger.

She should have clearly explained the situation: "I am so very sorry. I'm afraid I was being overzealous about our parking lot. The attendant is ill today and I just didn't recognize your car."

She also should have done whatever was necessary to rectify the situation, such as ordering a limousine for the client while she retrieved his car. The next day, sincere notes, both to the client and her boss, would have put her apology on record. And if things had cooled down by the following week and her boss and client were even joking a bit about the incident, she might try a little humor and creativity. A toy tow truck with a small gold plaque attached with the inscription, "To commemorate a most unfortunate incident, November 18, 1991," could have helped turn a disaster into an opportunity to show some presence and imagination. As it was, Helen told me she slunk back to work the next day, kept her door closed for the rest of the week, and felt inept and powerless.

AN OFFER THEY COULD REFUSE

I once spoke to a group of lawyers who were evaluating my professional image program for use in their law firm. When I finished a presentation that clearly showed how their firm would benefit from my services, most of the partners were smiling and nodding their heads, and everyone appeared to be in general agreement. Of course, I assured them that this program would simply be a refresher for them and that the people who really needed the course were their associates in three-piece polyester suits outside the conference room.

However, the senior partner, the one whose name appeared first on the door, peered at me through his reading glasses. In a most condescending tone, he proceeded to inform me that my program was something that parents and universities should have instilled. That certainly by the time one has become a lawyer with a large firm, these items of image are second nature. Eye contact, demeanor, moving with authority in front of a jury, and especially issues of clothing were too elementary to warrant serious discussion.

Immediately, all the heads in the room changed directions—from vertical to horizontal. The entire mood of the group went from positive to negative in about twelve seconds. There was no point in debating this issue because the senior partner was rising to his feet, and the meeting was over.

Of course, I was embarrassed and slightly humiliated. No one likes to be summarily dismissed, but I kept my composure, shook hands, smiled, and asked for some referrals. I kept telling myself that everyone who has stepped up to bat has struck out at one time or another.

When the meeting broke up, the senior partner and I headed to the restrooms at the same time. A few minutes later the situation was still strained as we both silently entered the elevator on the twentieth floor. Suddenly I noticed that, unknown to him, his fly was open. Since it was almost noon, the elevator stopped on each of the top ten floors, filling up steadily and forcing everyone closer together. As we stood packed in the elevator, a woman's fluffy boucle jacket caught on the senior partner's open zipper.

At that point he recognized that he had a problem, but he just stood there frozen and red-faced, at a loss about what to do. His fine breeding had deserted him. When we reached the lobby, the secretary shot out of the elevator, dragging her most unwilling partner behind her as he frantically tried to disengage himself from her clothing.

HANDLING EMBARRASSMENT

Most of us can think of many brilliant ways to handle an embarrassing situation once it is over. But to have the necessary presence of mind when the incident occurs is a learned skill.

The unfortunate senior partner should have spent the elevator time, once he realized that he was caught in the jacket, in either getting himself untangled or thinking of something hilarious to say.

Humor, especially self-deprecating humor, is often the best way to recover from an embarrassing moment. But when you simply can't think of anything funny to say, be matter-of-fact and businesslike. He could have tapped her on the shoulder and said, quite simply, "Excuse me, miss, but would you hold still for just a moment? I seem to be caught on your jacket."

PUTTING YOURSELF AND OTHERS AT EASE

An important characteristic of showing power and presence is the ability to put others at ease while appearing comfortable yourself.

Most people don't like to see someone else uncomfortable. They want the situation to return to normal as soon as possible.

Certainly if the situation warrants it, offer a brief apology. If you drop a fork full of eggroll with duck sauce on the boss's oriental rug at a cocktail party, for example, humor would be inappropriate. In a case like this, if you can rectify the problem immediately, do so. If not, offer to have it corrected later. Fussing and fuming too much will make everyone feel uneasy and undermine all the goodwill that is being created by the occasion.

By all means, even if no one saw you spill your coffee or break a wine glass, mention it to the proper person so that the stain can be treated or the broken glass swept up. If you accidently spill a soda on a client's copier, for example, tell someone immediately to avoid potential damage both to the equipment and the relationship.

If you drop your briefcase on your foot and it spills open, recover as smoothly as possible. Don't stop in mid-sentence and scramble around putting papers in order, and don't act horrified that you could be such a klutz. You shouldn't make your embarrassing moments embarrassing for everyone else, too.

In a case such as this one, finish your sentence, stay relaxed with your body language, and calmly kneel down and reassemble things. If the situation can wait to be cleaned up, wait. Never add to the confusion unless absolutely necessary.

REACTING TO SOMEONE ELSE'S EMBARRASSMENT

When another person is embarrassed, try to alleviate that individual's discomfort. Ignore the incident, brush it off as unimportant, and help the person to recover if possible.

In many cases, you can do a great deal to alleviate someone else's difficulty, and look more impressive for doing so. If a client knocks over a glass of water at a working lunch and the contents spill all over your report, try not to overreact. Immediate assurance that everything is all right and can be easily replaced is a demonstration of powerful and elegant behavior.

Sometimes it helps an embarrassed person's feelings if you relate a (preferably amusing) story about the time when you were embarrassed. You might say: "Don't feel bad. You should have seen me when I ordered iced tea with lemon. As I absentmindedly squeezed the lemon, it flew up in the air and landed on top of my head!"

IT'S A BIRD, IT'S A PLANE, IT'S . . .

When I started my company, in 1979, I called on a partner with one of the big accounting firms. I was intimidated by this executive who had twenty-five years as an extremely successful numbers man; he had put together some very impressive deals and was frequently quoted in the city's business magazines. He made it clear to me right away that he was doing me a favor . . . which he was.

Wardrobe-wise, he was extremely "together" with a custom-made Oxxford wool suit, Egyptian cotton shirt, and Bally shoes. The keys to his Mercedes were visible and so was the athletic bag behind his desk. He was Superman.

He had everything—including a false tooth that came flying out of his mouth in mid-conversation and landed on my file folder. He was absolutely mortified, and I didn't know what to do. No one had ever taught me the proper way to return someone's tooth.

We sat there for what seemed like an hour. Then I picked up his tooth and carefully put it on his desk next to his golf trophy while I continued to talk, never referring to the incident in any way.

He never really recovered, partly because of his embarrassment and partly because he didn't want to continue talking with a big gap in the front of his mouth.

He would have been better off if he had excused himself, replaced the tooth in private, and returned to continue the meeting. Or I should have indicated that I had another appointment and re-scheduled with him at a later date. A golden rule of professional presence is never to make the embarrassment greater than it already is. Even turning the tables and making the incident look like your fault can be a very generous and effective gesture.

LOSING POINTS WITH THE BOSS

In most cases, a boss is a boss—not a dear friend, not a close confidant, and not one to take lightly or flippantly. Although you may see each other daily and work closely together, you still have to adhere to a certain protocol that comes with such a relationship.

The most obvious mistake is to criticize your boss's decisions in front of others. Although you don't need to be a "yes-person," you need to select your confrontations carefully and always in private.

Several years ago, I was attending the launching of a new product at the annual meeting of an international cosmetics company. The new item had been in research and development for two years and was heralded as the product with the most growth potential in the entire line. After a spectacular multi-media presentation to the sales force by the president of the company, the new product was greeted with a standing ovation. But during the question-and-answer period, one of the district sales managers stood up and asked why the labeling was so confusing. He also wanted to know why such an unattractive model was chosen for the ad campaign.

In one fell swoop, he significantly dampened the enthusiasm that the president had worked so hard to create, and negated months of effort by the creative team. The other attendees began to mutter among themselves. The president abruptly cut off questions, and the meeting ended on an adverse note. The next day the district manager received an early morning phone call from his boss, saying that he was no longer needed in his position.

Unless there is an immediate remedy available, why create a no-win confrontation with the boss? Attacking the boss's decisions in public is certainly the surest way to jeopardize your position. Even a private discussion would have been nonproductive because this was not a planning meeting. This was a product launch where the only objective was to become enthused over the new product, not to embarrass the boss.

Other issues that create friction and may cause problems with the boss include:

- Ignoring an important social invitation from the boss.
- Getting drunk at a company function.
- Making a pass at a customer.
- Inviting the boss to social events with your close friends.
- Back slapping, arm grabbing, and any other physical contact other than a handshake.
- Insisting on discussing business in a purely social situation.
- Not deferring seating to him or her in a meeting.

- Expecting the boss to lug around the majority of the heavy equipment on a sales call or the luggage on a business trip.
- Wasting the boss's time with frequent tales of your many personal problems.

Positioning yourself professionally with your boss and others up the ladder means that you will come to mind when promotions, bonuses, and very visible special projects come up. Bosses know which employees to keep in the background and which to show off. Those with power and presence are showcased because the boss knows that they are dependable in any situation.

If you are unfortunate enough to have a really terrible and unfair boss, as we have all had at one time or another, it is still to your professional and personal advantage to afford your boss a level of respect. Maintaining your dignity and showing professionalism will not detract from your power. Even if, for example, you are forced to listen to a litany of marital woes from your boss, when he is the one having the extra-marital affairs, listen, don't offer advice, and then try to redirect the subject back to business.

BAD COMPANY

Companies, just like high schools, have both team players and troublemakers. Remember the kind of student who always caused trouble, bullying others, stirring up strife and lying to cover himself—the Eddie Haskell type?

Malcolm Zatt is Eddie all grown up. He is naturally self-destructive. Although he is above average in sales, he frequently cheats on his expense account when he travels, with acts as brazen as taking a load of dirty clothes with him on a trip to have them cleaned at the company's expense.

He also loves to take on the boss in staff meetings, seemingly for the sake of argument, and he never misses a chance to point out a colleague's error, making sure that everyone else hears him. The problem is that Malcolm has taken a liking to Thomas Wiggins, a rather quiet, hard-working product manager.

Malcolm invariably sits by Tom in meetings, making sarcastic comments under his breath and elbowing Tom when he wants to call attention to someone's blunder. The staff resents Malcolm, and they are unfortunately beginning to think of Malcolm and Tom as a team.

Tom realizes that Malcolm's reputation is rubbing off on him, but he doesn't know how to terminate the relationship without making Malcolm angry. Although Tom doesn't want him for an enemy, it's more risky to continue the friendship.

Friendships develop naturally when people work together. But when you sense that the association is going to be a bad one, like the Malcolm/Tom relationship, then it is time to decline lunch, tactfully to stay busy every night after work, and to seat yourself between two other people at meetings. Sooner or later the other person will get the message.

TURNING NEGATIVES INTO POSITIVES

Professional presence is never more important than when it sees us through both critical circumstances and sticky situations. The way we behave under difficulty can actually cause us to emerge in a better position than had the incident never occurred. When other people see us handle ourselves well under stress, they become aware of an added dimension to our professionalism. We aren't just a business facade; we display true depth.

True character reveals itself under pressure, and when we have the presence to behave well when things are falling apart, we should certainly shine in all other environments.

Business people have a universal admiration for those who are tough, directed, and cool when under the gun. Because our mettle has been tested under difficult situations, we can take comfort in knowing that our presence, power, and leadership will emerge even more strongly under normal business conditions.

Most situations are repairable. Whether we have called unfavorable attention to ourselves or embarrassed our boss, the way we recover and repair the incident will say a great deal about our character and abilities. Keep these occurrences in perspective. No one goes through a career without making blunders.

CHAPTER TWELVE

CONTEMPORARY MANNERS AND BUSINESS BEHAVIOR

A neighbor of mine who had accidently cut off another car when she entered the highway, became enraged when the whole carload of passengers made a rude hand gesture in unison. Their car had her company's emblem on the side so it was obvious where they worked. She sped up, got their license number, and reported them to personnel the minute she got to work.

When the driver was contacted, he admitted to what they had done and apologized. But she wanted written letters of apology from everyone who was in the car, and she wanted copies put in their personnel files.

When she told me about this, she added, "They were sure lucky that it was me they made this nasty gesture to. With someone else from the company, it would have been a lot worse."

My first reaction was to be extremely thankful that I was not an innocent passenger in the car who might have been compelled into going along with the crowd. The second was to recognize her as one of those people who was chronically unhappy with the way the world behaves.

We live in an imperfect world full of flawed human beings. People are sometimes rude. We can't always control their behavior. Self-righteously trying to correct every grievance is pointless and nonproductive. Pointing out every indiscretion, rudeness, and slight is a waste of time and energy. Seeking to rise above poor manners is a much easier way to live, and it also epitomizes power and presence.

Good manners are one of the hallmarks of professional presence. It is impossible to be considered sophisticated and competent without them. No matter what our background, whether our parents schooled us in etiquette or not, as professionals it is our obligation to fill in the blanks.

A CHAUVINIST PIG? I THINK NOT.

Gender issues are usually muddled for men and sometimes for women. One of the questions that is frequently raised in my seminars by male attendees is, "Can I show good manners to my female colleagues and clients without appearing sexist?" The answer is yes, yes, and again yes.

For most women, the issue is simply that we don't want to be regarded as a nuisance. When a speaker constantly makes reference to the sole female in the audience, that speaker is treating her in a way that makes the audience annoyed, and her a clear nuisance.

When I was pregnant and enjoying a coed exercise class, the instructor kept making reference to how I could modify a particular exercise due to my pregnancy. Two of the super jocks in front of me turned around and hissed, "I wish you weren't in this class. This added instruction is driving us nuts." I hadn't requested extra assistance from the instructor, but in an ill-conceived attempt to include me, he alienated his participants and made me the brunt of their resentment.

Speakers are notorious for being inadvertantly sexist. "Lady and Gentlemen" is a silly way to start a presentation. Constantly making reference to the one or two women in a seminar is a mistake. In a meeting, it is completely unnecessary for a male to say, "I want to tell an off-color joke, but I wouldn't want to offend the woman in our group." Either tell the joke or don't tell it, but don't make the woman responsible for your behavior.

Women also don't want to be regarded as people who need special assistance simply because of their gender. Good manners mean that we lend a helping hand when the situation warrants it without gender consideration. Helping someone on with their coat, holding a door, or offering to carry something is not gender specific.

If a woman feels that a gesture is truly superfluous, she can simply say with a warm smile, "Thank you, I can manage myself." This will be a clear indication that well-bred courtesies were offered and she has decided to decline them. But rarely will genuine courtesies ever be refused.

It is not advisable, however, to make a business encounter feel like a date. It is not necessary for a man to hold a chair for a female colleague, open and close her car door, or create any gratuitous physical contact.

HONEY, BABY, DARLIN'

It is never smart or useful to make a fuss in public over an unintentional gender mistake. A courtly older gentleman may rush to open the door for a woman, address her as ma'am, and maybe even slip with a "honey" or two.

As a woman, keep business objectives in mind. Accept the courtesies while keeping strong, no-nonsense eye contact and a straightforward but friendly manner. But don't smile too much. Gracefully handling this situation shows that you have a sense of when to and when not to make an issue of things.

As a man, it is safe to assume that business women will not readily respond to terms of endearment like "baby" and "sugar lump." As a woman, assume that most business men will not easily respond to "boy," "sweetie," or "pumpkin."

A PUBLIC MISTAKE

When I was a speaker at a sales award banquet, it surprised me to watch how saleswomen were greeted on stage versus how salesmen were acknowledged. When a woman walked on stage to accept her award for exceeding her sales quota, she was hugged, kissed, and generally treated like a blushing bride.

When a man accept the same award, his hand was shaken, his

award presented, and that was it. No hugging, no kissing. He was treated like a professional receiving an award for hard work.

Many of the attendees, both male and female, were up in arms after the ceremony because of the way the awards were handled. The implication was that the saleswomen had gotten to the top because of their femininity and good looks and the men through their hard work.

The master of ceremonies thought that he was showing warmth and good manners in greeting the female award winners with an embrace. What he didn't realize was that good manners dictated that he should have disregarded gender and treated everyone the same.

HUMOR—WITHIN THE BOUNDS OF GOOD TASTE

Humor can be a wonderful business tool and a way of lightening up the pressures of the workplace. It relaxes people and eases tensions along with aiding a number of involuntary physiological functions like reducing high blood pressure. Humor, however, must be used appropriately and within the bounds of good taste.

In business it is easy to let things get out of hand at a staff meeting or even a gab session in the hallway. Screeching and loud laughter are disruptive. Practical jokes are counterproductive.

I once entered a law office where the partners were crouched behind the chairs of the conference room shooting each other with squirt guns. They had just won a major case and this was their way of releasing tension and celebrating. Although I thought it was pretty funny, I also decided not to use that law firm.

Developing a sense of when to pull back and refocus on business is vital not only in showing good manners but also in maintaining power and control. To gain a reputation as the office clown without balancing this with a serious sense of direction is a mistake.

In my first job, one of my coworkers had a sense of humor that was consistently scatological and offensive. "Watch out for Number One and don't step in Number Two" was his trademark joke. He was rarely taken seriously at any staff meeting, and we were all nervous about having him meet our customers and vendors.

Managers in particular must be careful that their humor doesn't diminish the importance of a job, assignment, or a new product. In that kind of environment, hard work and dedication can feel almost foolish. Staying late to check figures and polish up a report seems a waste of time if the boss cracks a bad joke about it.

There is an etiquette to responding to jokes in business. If the joke is funny, laugh. If it's not funny, but not offensive, at least smile. No one ever tells a joke thinking it's not funny. If it's offensive, racist, or sexist, it is correct not to respond and to immediately change the subject.

It is also immature to make a stab at tomfoolery with "frat boy" humor. For example, I have sat through some rather dry presentations where the presenter tried to spice things up by including a few slides from the centerfold of *Playboy* magazine. Although this got a few chuckles at first, most people are offended at sophomoric humor.

HANDLING ANGER ON THE JOB

Professional presence means having credibility. We need for others to trust us and to feel our behavior is predictable. It's hard to trust or depend on someone who seems emotionally unstable and shows it through erratic gestures and uncontrolled outbursts.

Of course, everyone blows up from time to time. We all have our hot buttons. Some issues simply ignite us and can almost guarantee that our behavior will be emotional and generally unprofessional. We need to know what these issues are so that we can begin to control our responses.

If others see us react irrationally to a small matter, we will damage our power and influence with them. In such cases, we are perceived as less than professional, less able to handle ourselves. Temper tantrums rarely enhance stature.

Business professionals who begin to use foul and vulgar language whenever they are upset are easily pegged. They are making their anger obvious and transparent. It is easy to gauge their level of emotional instability by the number of times they swear in each sentence.

Similarly, the man or woman who gets teary-eyed when a manager or a client doesn't like his or her work is seriously jeopardizing a career. We are all entitled to an occasional cry at work, but with the door shut. Crying is an emotional display that never wins points or admiration, and crying out of frustration is far different than crying from a devastating personal or national tragedy.

I'M MAD AS HELL AND I'M NOT GOING TO TAKE IT ANYMORE

Know your "anger and frustration triggers." Identify what turns you into a raving maniac. Awareness can then leads to a more responsible reaction.

Fourteen Surefire Anger Triggers

1. Having a boss or coworker regularly critique your appearance.
2. Being stood up for an appointment.
3. Being unfairly criticized without the opportunity to respond.
4. Being deliberately lied to.
5. Discourteous treatment of your secretary.
6. Watching a coworker show flagrant disregard of established rules.
7. Always being asked to do the "household chores."
8. Working with someone who refuses to admit mistakes.
9. Dealing with someone who constantly interrupts you in meetings and conversations.
10. Having an associate finish your sentences.
11. Enduring habitual lateness.
12. Listening to endless chatter about subjects not related to business.
13. Having a confidence betrayed.
14. Having someone make you look inept, uninformed, or stupid in front of others.

There are many effective ways to respond to problems other than by getting angry, frustrated, or emotional. Here are three methods of handling your own anger on the job while maintaining presence.

STYLE ONE: THE STONE FACE

Rather than getting defensive and angry, don't react at all. Keep all signs of anger under wraps. When we observe some of our greatest business leaders, many, under circumstances of great anger, remain controlled. "The less said the better" is their style.

Of course, you can't keep anger pent up forever. It's not healthy. But choose the right way to deal with it. You can deal with the offender in private, vent your anger through exercise, or pour out your soul to a close, nonbusiness-related friend.

STYLE TWO: THE PATIENT FACE

Sometimes in a flash of anger we react too quickly. We don't stop to listen or to let others finish their sentences. Something may hit us where we are vulnerable, and we check out of the logical, predictable world and travel on pure emotion.

If we can be patient and wait for the right moment, our anger can be clearly directed and channeled effectively. Our body language can still obviously state that we are extremely displeased, but in waiting to respond verbally, we create a strong image. Once again, we appear to be in control.

The old trick of counting to ten can be very powerful. Sit or stand perfectly still. Look the person in the eye with an unblinking stare for several seconds. When you do begin to speak, speak slowly and quietly, carefully weighing your words. Make others strain a little to hear you. The air will absolutely crackle with intensity, and your assailant will be put uncomfortably off balance. If your assailant is your boss, the same advice will help you maintain your dignity.

STYLE THREE: THE CLOWN FACE

Often, you can help yourself by putting the situation in perspective. Stop and say to yourself, "This isn't a deal-breaker." Poking a little fun at yourself and the circumstances will help you feel better, and everyone around you will be put at ease in a hurry.

WHEN YOU'RE ON THE RECEIVING END OF ANGER OR CRITICISM

Class is often defined as grace under pressure. In every business person's life, there comes a time when we each suffer some type of business humiliation. Depending on the business, it may happen more than once. There are a number of ways to react, most of which just worsen the problem.

Here is a list of the ways not to react to criticism:

1. Make excuses. "I haven't been feeling well lately, and you just keep making me work late. It's no wonder that I botched that project. I'm just exhausted."

2. Cry. "I know you don't like me. You have never taken me or my work seriously. You love to humiliate me in front of the office and make me cry."

3. Counterattack. "Well, I may not have gotten this report in on time, but at least I didn't get drunk and make a fool of myself at the last company picnic!"

The best way to defend yourself is often a completely straightforward, sincere apology. It will go a long way in rectifying the situation. Once you state, "I'm sorry. It's my fault," the discussion usually ends. When you step up and accept the blame for your behavior, others aren't so quick to blame or criticize you.

WHEN YOU ARE ATTACKED PUBLICLY

Sometimes we are the object of a public attack and we can't really fight back. Not everyone has a good boss with a sense of timing, and certainly we can't control a public dressing down by a client or customer.

One of the best strategies for dealing with a situation in which you feel you have very little control is to use nonverbal behavior. If someone attacks you during a presentation and it would be too awkward to get up and leave, look the person squarely in the eye, hold the look for a moment, and then pick right back up. Then your message becomes, "I heard you, but what you are saying is so off track and uncalled for that I choose not to deal with it." You will keep control of the situation and actually enhance your own power.

Reacting without having time to construct your case can be a mistake. Why get dragged into an unfriendly arena? In the heat of the moment, the less said the better. Showing little or no reaction can actually take the wind out of an angry sail, and you will end up the better player with more poise and presence. You can always reintroduce the issue later, with just the two of you, when tempers are more under control.

If a colleague, a superior, or sometimes even a customer has criticized you in public, it is always possible to take him or her aside later and to quietly say: "Please don't criticize me in public. If you have any criticism to make, tell me about it privately." Most bullies are so taken aback by a straightforward approach that they often change their behavior immediately.

Although discussing issues in private poses the least amount of conflict, this doesn't mean that you allow outright lies or misrepresentations to go publically unchallenged. If the situation is critical to your integrity and other people are present, you may have to respond right then and there.

"Mike, you are misinformed. We did not let you down. We did not commit to a September fifteenth deadline because we need at least two weeks to ship, even on a rush order. This order wasn't even signed by you until September twelfth."

But choose carefully when to take up the gauntlet and when to let the other person just rant and play out the anger. An angry person is the one who is losing control. Often, the calmer you remain, the more absurd the other person appears. If you refuse to be drawn into the fray, your opponent looks increasingly ridiculous.

WHO ASKED YOUR OPINION, ANYWAY?

You can never go wrong by not offering unsolicited advice. This is true in the office as well as at social events. Even solicited advice is tricky. When someone asks what you think about their new office furniture, they usually don't want negative feedback no matter what they say. If you think it looks tacky, why say anything?

The only time to call negative attention to someone's appearance or behavior is if they can do something about it immediately. Quietly mentioning that they have barbecue sauce on their forehead is a kind remark. Most people will feel grateful. Telling someone that their suit is much too tight or that their hairpiece looks like "road kill" is unnecessary.

In business conversation, is it correct to point out errors that other people have made? Of course. Data must be accurate and information clear. But this should be done without making the offender feel defensive. "I think you have those figures wrong, Fred. Let me show you what I have," is much better than, "Wrong, wrong, wrong, you knucklehead. You always mess up those weekly sales figures."

CONSIDERATION IN THE OFFICE

One of my clients complained that she was amazed at how unschooled her new recruit was in office protocol and basic consideration. She had scheduled a meeting with him for one o'clock and he kept her waiting until 1:30 P.M. because he had to drive home and "put the dog out."

"I know that he was being truthful in telling me why he was late, but I couldn't believe that he expected me to appreciate the fact that his dog took precedence over a meeting with me, his new boss. It was an immediate indicator to me to look for other problems. If he demonstrated such inconsiderate behavior toward me now, how was he going to treat our customers?"

Subsequently my client had a private conversation with her associate and pointed out his lack of consideration. She told him that his attitude and manners were just as important to the company as the actual dollars that he generated because, in fact, one lead to the other.

Being inconsiderate can also take the form of telling a business associate personal information that will make them resentful.

Reporting to the harried receptionist that you will be gone for three hours because you are going to exercise and then enjoy a full body massage is tactless. If you are leaving the office for some type of personal enjoyment, even during your lunch hour, it's a breech of good office etiquette to create potential resentment by revealing your destination to someone who doesn't have the same opportunity.

WHERE THERE'S SMOKE . . .

The etiquette of smoking today is simple. Don't do it in front of other people. It used to be a shared experience—a meeting over a cup of coffee and a cigarette—but no more. Smoking in public is almost like using a toothpick; it is best done in the restroom or alone.

"Seven Misfires in the Smoking Arena"

1. Don't smoke in a conference room, even if others are.
2. Don't smoke in a client's office, even if they are doing so.
3. Never smoke in someone else's car.
4. Don't smoke in restaurants, even in the smoking section, unless everyone else is smoking at your table, too.
5. Don't smoke in your own car if you are heading to an important appointment. The odor will be very apparent even if your windows are rolled down. Many sales managers who have salespeople who travel mostly by car, caution their people not to smoke at all in the car. The odor on the clothes and the breath of a smoker is the first thing that "hits" a customer when that sales person walks in.

6. Don't wear the same suit the day after you have gone to a smokey bar. Even if you don't smoke and even if you air out the suit for eight hours, yours will smell of smoke.

7. Don't miss washing your hair after an evening with smokers because it will retain the odor.

If you do smoke, you are obviously not a criminal. You have the right to do it. Just use the utmost courtesy in business situations.

ATTITUDE ADJUSTMENT

Whatever you do in the name of business, whatever courtesies you extend, must be offered with integrity and not grudgingly. Your enthusiasm and graciousness must be genuine.

If you find that you really dislike doing business with obese people, women, gays, or other minorities and that your manner and attitude reflect that, you need an attitude adjustment. Aside from being fair, it's just good business.

If loud people, womanizers, flirts, whiners, or macho men really annoy you, deal with your feelings first. We are able to select our friends. We usually don't have the opportunity to select our customer base. The success of our business encounters will depend on our ability to make a genuine connection without hostile or condescending undercurrents.

Good manners are not just reserved for those who share the same values. In a business relationship, courtesies need to be extended to everyone. Find a way to put aside your judgments and seek an authentic area of mutual interest or concern.

Roberta Langford is a well-educated colleague of mine who was raised in a rather privileged and sheltered background. As a sales engineer for a large chemical company, she often has to take out a group of unsophisticated manufacturer's representatives who tend to discuss women's anatomy and violent movies over dinner.

She used to dread their monthly visits but was usually unsuccessful in getting out of the obligation. So she decided to do something about it.

The first thing she made herself do was mentally to place her poor attitude in the glove compartment of her car before walking into the restaurant. Second, she mentally placed a large sign around the neck of each man that said, "I am a caring, concerned human being."

Third, she took charge of the conversation by asking her customers questions until she found something that they all enjoyed discussing. As it turned out, two of the men felt as strongly as she did about the importance of preserving the environment. In fact, one of them had organized a neighborhood recycling center.

Finding this area of mutual interest surprised her. She now sincerely looks forward to spending the evening together with them when they're in town.

They even confided to her that the only reason they used to have dinner with her was to get a free meal. They had perceived her as stuffy and arrogant. Now that they found out that she was spending one Saturday a month picking up trash along the highway, she was a "regular guy" to them. Roberta decided, because of this experience, that if she was going to consider herself a professional, she should be able to show presence and a level of graciousness whether or not she liked a client personally.

GOOD MANNERS ARE NOT A MEANINGLESS RITUAL

Etiquette, for etiquette's sake, is empty activity and a meaningless ritual. But genuine good manners and a working knowledge of professional behavior are essential and productive business skills. Good manners will humanize and harmonize a business relationship and promote a powerful spirit of cooperation in our work environments.

Part V

◆

BREAKING BREAD AND BUILDING BONDS: ENTERTAINING AND TRAVEL

CHAPTER THIRTEEN

THE BUSINESS MEAL: DINING AND DEALING

The business meal has taken on all forms. It no longer needs to be the three-hour lunch at The Club. It can also be a hot dog shared in the park, a cocktail party where contacts are made, a succinct breakfast, or a formal dinner. But the objective is not to see how much or how often you can eat at your company's expense. The objective is to develop relationships.

A friend of mine who is a stockbroker invites clients to lunch and often orders only vichyssoise. This cold potato soup is elegant and can't cool off because it is served chilled. He usually grabs a sandwich going back to the office, but during his lunch, he has been able to focus fully on his client.

Part of developing relationships is knowing what to do and how to do it. Part of effective dining is to illustrate innate good manners. That is why it is difficult to eat like an animal at home and expect to adapt a different set of manners in public.

The comfort of picking up the phone, setting up a meal, and eating together further cements a relationship. Simply put, we do business with people we know.

Does dining together grease the wheel of commerce? Of course! Why else would the IRS allow a business deduction for entertainment? But to create presence, business dining must be done with style, savvy, and sophistication.

BREAKFAST MEETINGS: THE EARLY BIRD TAKES CONTROL

Breakfast is an ingenious way to build business relationships. It is less expensive, both in money and in time. It fits into people's schedules more easily than do lunches and dinners. It doesn't carve into the business day. It is a peppy, energizing, and upbeat way to do business. Most business people will commit to a breakfast meeting, whereas they might decline a lunch or dinner.

Hotel coffee shops or dining rooms are usually the best places to meet because they are less crowded, parking is easier, and the tables have tablecloths, which lends a little more elegance than cracked Formica.

I have chaired a number of committees and found that breakfast meetings were the best times to get maximum attendance. There is a natural attraction to the image of scrambled eggs and cheese, crisp bacon, and hot buttered biscuits, even if the reality is more like a low-cholesterol spread on wheat toast. More than any other meal, people love breakfast.

There is a certain dynamic quality to people who regularly schedule breakfast meetings. They are on the fast track and prefer to wake up an hour early to meet a client, rather than spend two hours at lunch when they could be making sales calls and working on the phone. Most power breakfasters eat lunch on the run; with breakfast they will already have satisfied their desire for a sit-down meal.

Breakfast at a fast-food restaurant is such a slice of Americana. It humanizes a corporate life on the road when we see moms, kids, and blue collar folks. It is a quick and efficient way to meet colleagues to discuss a new project. It can also be a change of pace for a breakfast business meeting with well-established customers, and it is certainly more economical than other alternatives.

THE LUNCH CRUNCH

Lunch is still the most popular business meal. But the timing has changed. Rule number one—avoid the crunch. Try scheduling lunch at an odd hour so you won't waste time fighting the crowds or schedule it at a restaurant that takes lunch reservations. Although only higher-priced restaurants will take reservations at midday, it is worth paying a little more for the security of knowing you won't be hanging around the lobby for twenty minutes wasting a client's time. And be sure to dine at a restaurant before you take a customer there.

Try to frequent the same restaurant regularly because you will be familiar with the menu selections, the best table, the restrooms, and the telephones. You will also have had an opportunity to introduce yourself to the maître d', who will then be able to greet you on subsequent visits by name. If you can find a good restaurant that is owned and personally managed by the proprietor, there is an added feeling of warmth, comfort, and familiarity.

If you belong to a club, you will generally be guaranteed a good table with the leisure to extend the lunch if you need to. Many clubs offer "lunch only" privileges for a much lower initiation fee.

Don't talk business until everyone has looked at the menu, decided what they want, and ordered. Otherwise you will be constantly interrupted and your effectiveness will be diminished. As the host or hostess, take charge of the lunch and instruct the waitperson when you want to order.

Save the most important business information for after the main entree. Over coffee and dessert, weighty topics get more attention than between forkfuls of a roast beef platter. Learn to answer a question with a bit of food in your mouth. It is exasperating to dine with someone who will speak only when they have a completely empty mouth.

Liquor at lunch is passé. In fact ordering hard liquor at lunch creates the image of a person with a drinking problem. Wine or beer should be the "hardest" liquids at noonday.

DINING LEISURELY

Business dinners are the most gracious way to develop a business relationship. They are generally much more leisurely than lunch, and often extend to three hours. They allow the time and opportunity to discuss much more than business. When someone enjoys your company enough to suggest dinner, you have been paid a compliment.

But there are three dangers inherent in a dinner, as opposed to breakfast, lunch, or tea. The first is the open-ended aspect of the evening meal. When does it end? The second issue is that liquor is almost always involved. The third is that dinner is the closest thing to a date without being a date, so the ambiguity can be dangerous.

The first issue can be comfortably resolved with an invitation that involves not only what time dinner is, but also a reference to the fact that the restaurant is casual and not formal. That immediately indicates that the evening won't be drawn out with various courses. You can also make a reference to your client's tight schedule and promise an early evening.

If you have weighty business issues to discuss, try to do it at the bar or in the dining room prior to dinner. Dinner is different from lunch. It's more of a social event. It is very difficult to relax, exchange family anecdotes and fishing tips and then hit a client with a price increase.

Unless you are an extremely smooth negotiator, don't try to soften a customer's defenses and then sock them with hard issues. This feels like a breach of trust. In fact, depending on the success of the dinner, you may decide to forego serious business entirely and just establish a relationship. You can always follow up with a business meeting in their office the following day.

After specific issues have been discussed, order dinner, enjoy an after-dinner coffee but forego any bar hopping afterwards. Baby-sitters and early morning meetings are always an excuse, if you really feel you need one to end an evening.

The issue of drinking can become sticky. It is always acceptable not to drink. But it is not acceptable to make someone feel uncomfortable if they enjoy drinking. With no further business commitments at the end of the day, this is the most logical time to imbibe.

One of my female clients who owns a manufacturing company, has customers who love to drink, especially if she is picking up the tab. They always want to meet at the bar and it becomes a protracted and very liquid interlude to dinner.

She has solved this by quietly telling the bartender, after thirty minutes, to keep pouring drinks if they are requested, but with a minute amount of liquor. She also tries to invite her customers to restaurants other than at their hotel. They are generally more responsible in their drinking because they know they can't just stagger onto the elevator and flop into bed.

To keep a business dinner from looking like a date, spouses are sometimes invited just to make certain that the intent is clear. It is also a nice compliment to the spouse. However, the whole flavor of a meeting changes when spouses are involved and the event becomes almost purely social.

So how does a business dinner stay that way? For starters, don't hold a chair for your client. That looks and feels like a date. Ask for a quiet table, but not one in the dark. Stay away from restaurants that are traditionally enjoyed by lovers. You know the kind . . . cozy, warm, and intimate. Don't share food or drink.

One of my single, male clients in California has a designated female business companion whom he invites whenever he has asked a female customer to dinner. He always tells his guest that someone from the office will be accompanying him. "I know I sound like a coward, Susan, but for me the dinner goes much smoother with my female colleague accompanying me and there is never any concern over ambiguities."

GOOD ADVICE FOR ANY MEAL

Don't spend a great deal of time scrutinizing the menu. If you have a hard time making a decision about what kind of soup you want, the question becomes, "Can this person make a decision in business?"

Don't take any medications in front of clients, especially those for a nervous stomach, ulcer, or a headache. If you need to take medicine, excuse yourself or wait until they excuse themselves.

Don't be overly conversational with the waitperson. Be friendly and polite, but diffusing the attention from your client to the person delivering your food is not good form.

Don't select exactly the same thing that a new client orders. It may look obsequious. At least order a different salad dressing, vegetable, or dessert. Although it is usually flattering for clients to see that you share the same tastes in food, be careful that at the first dining experience together, you don't appear like a sycophant.

Don't order soup unless you can eat it quietly and without spilling. Don't order pasta, triple-decker BLTs, huge, juicy hamburgers, corn on the cob, or anything that is eaten with the fingers. If a food selection can not be attractively eaten, don't order it during a business meal.

Take command but don't present a laundry list of topics to cover that you just give cursory attention to and then jump on to the next one. The whole reason to dine together is to establish a comfortable, trusting relationship. Racing from one thing to the next doesn't build a relationship. You will look insecure and pushy.

As the host of a business meal, it is up to you to make sure that the level of service is there for everyone. Inquire as to the quality of their food, and make sure you and your guest don't get hung out to dry with slow service. As the host or hostess, you should be the one to get a missing fork, to request additional rolls or more hot coffee for your guests.

When entertaining clients, always order the same progression of food so that they won't be eating alone. If you generally don't order an appetizer and salad and the client does, then order just one of the initial courses and keep it during their appetizer and salad. If you know you will be stuffed by the time the entree comes, or you are watching your weight, don't eat much. But at least have something in front of you. It is always awkward to eat when no one else is eating, so don't make your client feel ill at ease dining alone.

The host or hostess should always order last. Then you can take your customer's lead and order accordingly. If the guest orders liquor, the host should order something to drink, but it doesn't have to be alcoholic. If your guest declines liquor, the host or hostess generally does the same.

When coffee is served, request the check and confirm whatever follow-up commitments will be necessary. Do check the bill on a quick basis. Mentally do the arithmetic ahead of time so that you have some idea of the bill. If the amount is wrong, quietly excuse yourself to the front desk and discuss it out of earshot of your guests.

The word TIP comes from "To Insure Promptness." Tip money was originally placed on the table prior to a customer being served. If you want really wonderful service, tip prior to ordering, but do it so that no one sees you.

Everyone knows that tipping is optional but expected in the United States. Twenty percent for good service and a low total is appropriate. If your lunch was $5 and you received good service, leave a $1 (20%) tip. If your dinner tab was $300, the restaurant was casual, and you received good service, it is perfectly appropriate to leave $45 (15%)

because of the large amount of the bill. Round off the amount to the nearest quarter (or dollar if the amount is over $50) and tip on the pretax amount.

For very formal dining the following guide is appropriate:

- $5 to $20 to the concierge or maitre d' if you received an exceptional table, you want to make a favorable impression, or you received special consideration. Give the money in a handshake as you are seated or as you leave.
- 5% to the captain—added into the total bill. You will recognize the captain because this is the person who takes your order, cooks tableside, and sometimes presents the bill. The captain receives only 5% because he supervises six to eight waiters.
- 15% to the waiter—added into the total bill. The waiter serves your food and beverages and attends to special requests including supervising the busboy.
- $3 to $6 dollars to the wine steward or sommelier for each bottle of wine. If there is no room on the charge slip to add this, then it can be done with a handshake.

You can also write the dollar amount of 20% of the total bill over the blanks on the credit card where the captain's tip and the waiter's tip are. Then the service people are responsible for dividing up the amount.

ADDITIONAL TIPPING

- $1 to the ladies' room attendant
- $1 per coat to coat-room attendant

- $1 to doorman for summoning your car or getting a cab
- $1 to $2 to the parking-lot attendant. It is a great show of elegance and personal power to walk clients to their car and then tip the attendant for them. I have a female client who does this regularly for her male customers and they are always quite flattered.

GETTING TAKEN FOR A RIDE

If you extend an invitation to a client or customer, it is normally expected that you pick up the bill. However if your guest is adamant about paying for their own portion, quietly agree and just split it. The easiest way is to offer two credit cards.

Gender has absolutely nothing to do with who pays the bill. If you want to pay and anticipate a battle, arrive early, give your waiter your credit card imprint, and insist that they not allow your guest to pay.

If you are having lunch with colleagues, each pays for their own. If everyone generally orders the same thing, just split the bill evenly. Take charge. Pick up the bill, look at the amount, and quietly announce what each person should contribute, which should always include tax and tip. If the meals were extremely disproportionate in cost, try to take that into consideration. But if someone had an extra drink or an appetizer, just be gracious and split evenly.

Many colleagues just take turns picking up the tab. One person picks up the whole amount for one lunch, and the next lunch tab is picked up by the other. The key here is trust, knowing that your generosity will be reciprocated at a later date.

One company that I work with has an unspoken agreement with their vendors that they take turns picking up the check at the various trade show dinners. Since the tabs are usually around $600, everyone remembers who picked up the last one. My client paid for the March show and when everyone reconvened for May, the vendors disappeared when the bill came. After three cups of after-dinner coffee the check was still on the table, and although the vendors did come back, they didn't even attempt to pick up the check.

It finally got so awkward that my client just paid the bill, but very grudgingly. He didn't want to risk losing their business, but they had violated an important rule and broken the trust that had previously been there. And sadly, the main reason for breaking bread together, which is to build relationships, had turned into bad feelings and resentment. The next time they met at a trade show, my client declined the vendor's dinner invitation.

If the check sits there staring at you and your meal mate, and you assumed that you were the guest, you have two options. First, you can just pick up the check and pay the whole amount. Second, you can pick up the bill, and quietly announce, "Well, why don't we split this."

I was asked out to lunch at a very expensive restaurant several years ago by a woman who wanted me to help her develop her business. She wanted my advice on the feasibility of her business, she wanted to brainstorm, and she wanted the names of my clients, accountant, lawyer, and board members. I spent two hours helping her develop a business plan.

When the check came, she pushed it over to me saying, "Well, you sure are more successful than I am right now. So I'll get the next one." I paid it, but I felt abused. What I should have said with a wise smile was, "My dear, there is no free lunch. I think this is yours."

EXITING WITH GRACE

If you are with someone who is thoroughly enjoying themselves and doesn't seem to want to wind things up, then ask for the check, pay it, stand up and say, "It was such a pleasure having lunch (or dinner) with you and I am looking forward to doing it again." You are under no obligation to indicate you have another, pressing matter or another client waiting for you in your office.

Graciously end the meal and don't go into explanations. Busy people in business realize that a lunch or breakfast doesn't extend past one and a half to two hours. Dinner should wind up after two and a half to three hours.

NO CONSPICUOUS CONSUMPTION—
EXCEPT WHEN IT'S NECESSARY

If a business meal is for relationship building, or celebrating with clients because you have closed a big deal, don't go to the priciest restaurant and order the most expensive wine or champagne. You will look as though you are trying to bribe the client, that you charge too much money for your product, or that you don't have much loyalty to your company. Conspicuous consumption went out with the 1980s.

However, in metropolitan areas and when crowds and parking will be difficult, consider reserving a limousine for the evening. Although it may sound like a luxury, a limousine will allow you and your guests to arrive safe, dry (if it is raining), and on time.

The junior person or host always takes the jump seat or whatever is left after everyone else has gotten in. Limousines are generally charged to credit cards with a 15% tip added.

TIPS FOR A COCKTAIL/NETWORKING PARTY

1. Don't overload your plate. Pick out your favorite items and then just nibble. If you are extremely hungry, find an out-of-the-way seat, eat, and then resume mingling. And don't complain about the food, the drinks, or the decor. Stay away from foods that are hard to eat or sticky like honeyed chicken wings or anything with a messy sauce.

2. If you are standing up, don't try to eat and drink at the same time.

3. Hold your beverage in your left hand so that your right hand will not be wet, cold, and clammy to shake.

4. If you are talking to someone who is constantly scanning the room, move on to someone else.

5. Don't spend more than five or ten minutes with anyone. The idea of a cocktail party is to mix and mingle. You can always excuse yourself to get a drink or go to the restroom.

6. It is easier to attend a networking session if you go with someone you know. Just don't stay with that person all night. Otherwise, you have defeated the purpose of the event.

7. Be respectful of personal space. Don't stand closer than three feet to someone else unless the room is very crowded. Everyone likes to maintain their bubble of personal space.

8. When meeting a celebrity or highly placed executive, take the

initiative to greet them. Often a cocktail event is the only time we have access to high-ranking people. But don't overstay your welcome. Introduce yourself, say a few words, and then move on. Don't monopolize their time.

IT'S NOT LEMONADE, IT'S THE FINGERBOWL

Table manners are mostly a matter of practice and commonsense. But here are some that may not be so apparent.

- The napkin goes on the lap as soon as everyone is seated. Never tuck it into the waistband or anchor it on a button.
- A formal table setting will give the diner an introduction to what will be served. A cocktail fork, soup spoon, a flat, notched fish knife, and a dessert fork all foretell things to come.
- When presented with a formal table setting, always start from the outside utensils and work to the inside.
- In deciding what salad belongs to you and which roll to eat, remember that solids are placed on the left. Liquids like coffee, tea, wine, and cocktails are on the right. If you have ever eaten at a crowded table, you know how easy it is to eat someone else's roll or drink from the wrong water glass.
- Wine glasses are routinely picked up if they are not used. But the only glass that is removed during the meal is the sherry glass.
- Crisp bacon, asparagus, artichokes, olives, hors d'oeuvres, and crudities (raw vegetables) are properly eaten with the fingers.

- Shrimp cocktail is not cut into smaller pieces. Spear each piece with the cocktail fork and nibble.
- Bread is rarely served at a formal dinner, partly because there is already so much food and you don't want to fill up on bread. But if it is served and there is no bread and butter plate, then it is permissible to place the roll on the tablecloth.
- Never do more than gently wipe your nose in public. Anything more enthusiastic should be done alone.
- It is not garish to eat the garnish on your plate.

RELATIONSHIP BUILDING

Taking the time to cultivate business relationships through the breaking of bread will build bonds. When we connect on a more personal basis, when we let others know that we value them enough to spend extra time with them, trust is created and business gets completed.

CHAPTER FOURTEEN

BUSINESS ENTERTAINING AT HOME

Who has time to invite clients, bosses, or coworkers to their home? Who has time to clean up the house, plan the menu, shop, arrange for childcare, and then make sure everyone is happy, comfortable, and enjoying themselves at your soiree?

Not many people. That is why entertaining at home is such a uniquely wonderful way to make your customers or colleagues feel like very valued individuals. It is a lost art. Since we haven't done it for so long, or we have never done it at all, it can seem like an overwhelming, forbidding, and anxiety-producing event. Why put ourselves through it?

Yet every time we invite business associates to our apartment, condo, cabin, farm, or house in the suburbs, something positive happens. Everyone lets down the business guard and we get to know each other on very different terms. It is more personal, more relationship building, and more flattering than any request to dine even at the finest restaurant.

There is something about being invited to someone's home that is unlike any other invitation. A table in a restaurant belongs to whoever is seated there at the time. It is transient and temporary. Someone's home is permanent. It shows their taste, their hobbies or interests, their preference for books, music, colors, gardening, cooking, and all the other things that give richness and fullness to life. Extending an invitation to clients or colleagues for a home event shows that they feel safe and secure enough to share another part of their life.

But when is it appropriate? When can you invite a coworker over for dinner? How about a boss? Is it smart to invite customers?

Here are the answers.

HAVING THE BOSS TO DINNER

Inviting your boss to your home is either intriguing you right now or seems totally out of the question. Let's be honest. If your direct boss is a very refined, multi-millionaire, and you tend toward a rather eclectic look combining Pier One Imports with garage sale and flea market items, you would probably feel very uncomfortable extending an invitation to your home.

But if you are comfortable that there won't be a huge disparity between your environments, take the initiative, once you have already received an invitation from your boss to his or her home. The admonition here is generally to wait until your boss has already felt comfortable opening another dimension of his or her life to you.

One of my client reports, "As a boss, I am always very impressed when an employee invites me for dinner; I know they have worried about what to serve, how to serve it, and if will it be fancy enough. I admire their efforts and like getting to know them better on their terms."

I suggested to one of my seminar attendees that he consider inviting his boss over for a casual barbecue after my attendee expressed an interest in getting to know his boss better. Of course, I couldn't guarantee that the boss would accept, but the guidelines generally are to ask once and gauge the reaction. If the invitation is put off indefinitely, don't ask again. If you are extended a sincere raincheck, then ask again. If you receive an acceptance, feel honored.

DINNER, DANCING, OR DRINKS?

There is a big difference between having someone over for dinner and planning a genuine party around a theme. A dinner requires a five- to seven-day verbal invitation. It's more spontaneous and requires much less planning. You will also have the opportunity to get to know someone on a more personal basis over dinner at your house.

If you don't want to commit to a whole evening at your home, invite the boss, customer, or coworker over for hors d'oeuvres and drinks. If it is a client, you will always have something to share and discuss on a nonbusiness level.

Also, inviting someone just for drinks and appetizers won't tie you up cooking and serving. You will be able to concentrate on them during dinner out.

Generally if you are single, be judicious in inviting another single business person to your home. You don't want it to look like something it isn't. However, there are exceptions.

When I was with a cosmetics company, an executive search firm approached me and wanted to meet with me personally. Since I had a close friend in the business, I knew that one of her pet peeves was how a potential recruit would make reservations at the most expensive restaurant in town, just to get a free meal. I decided to take another approach. I wasn't in it for free food; I wanted a better position. Just because the recruiter was male was no reason in my book not to show some initiative.

I cooked a simple Southern meal, served it nicely, but kept everything very straightforward. Nothing was close to being even slightly romantic. I kept the lights on at nearly full power and the music upbeat. Although I didn't get the job and never saw him again, I coincidentally met his wife ten years later at one of my seminars. The reason she knew my name, although we had never met, was simple. She said that of all the hundreds of people that her husband had worked to recruit, he never forgot that I was the only one who ever served him dinner, not the other way around. It was a nice way to be remembered!

If you are single, you also have the option of inviting someone else from your office, to buffer the situation. Also, if you have been with a client the entire day, it is nice to have the infusion of a new person. It also helps establish your company on a more solid footing because of the exposure to two people from the office.

One of my clients, who just recently started working with international businesses, decided to invite two male clients from Brazil along with their spouses. My client told me that she was extremely nervous because of the cultural differences. She also didn't speak Portuguese, although they spoke English fairly well.

As my client began serving the food, one of her clients asked,

"Diane, would you like some help?" Thinking how nice it would be to have two more hands, she replied, "Why yes, thank you." With that he looked at his wife and snapped his fingers and said, "Help her."

In amazement, she watched his obedient wife follow her into the kitchen. Since it wasn't in anyone's best interest to try and change Brazilian customs and attitudes that evening, she graciously accepted the help.

When dinner was over, her client looked at Diane and said, "Now, it's time for the men to work." He and the other client proceeded to clear the table, scrape the plates, load the dishwasher, scrub the pots, and completely clear the kitchen counters. Diane and the wives sat down and had a ball watching the men in the kitchen.

My client Diane is a fun-loving type and she stole away and got her camera. As she started taking pictures, the two clients started hamming it up and mugging for the camera. The wives were feeding Diane verbiage in Portuguese, which included, "Very good job," "Keep it up," and then, "Mop the floor and now clean the oven, too." She had no idea what she was telling them, but she repeated the words loudly and with gusto.

The wives ended up getting the last laugh with their little charade, and this event and the pictures that accompanied it have been passed around both companies. Over five hundred people from each firm know the story. A client dinner at home turned into an event that bonded not only five people but two large international companies.

A LITTLE OUT OF THE ORDINARY

Here is a list of ideas that may spark your interest in getting together with business associates.

1. Try grilling out German wieners and adding other German food for a Deutchland night.
2. Fondue gets people talking.
3. Try a bingo party with lots of booby prizes.
4. Do a Mexican party with a piñata, enchiladas, and mariachi music. Be sure to play "La Bamba!"
5. Try an Hawaiian party with flower or plastic leis, scooped out pineapples with fruit, and island music in the background.
6. Buy beer, make pizzas, and rent a copy of *Mystic Pizza*.
7. Plan a party around the last episode of a favorite television show. When "St. Elsewhere" aired its last program, I invited ten of my favorite clients and had hospital masks and several Playschool doctor's kits on hand. The pictures from that little gathering were wonderful and everyone received a framed group picture. This party took me ninety minutes to organize and it was a quick but lively pick-me-up in the middle of the business week.

A PARTY THEY WILL NEVER FORGET

A party, as opposed to dinner, requires much more time and preparation. It should be done around a theme that can be either an event, like the Super Bowl, or a murder mystery night, or a celebration because a new family room or deck was added to the house.

Personally, I do parties at the drop of a hat. I need only the smallest amount of encouragement to plan a party that will include friends, colleagues, and clients. My best parties have been those that commemorate a decade or a party from the past.

My '50s party, '20s party, and toga party were the best ones. One of my more staid clients showed up with a toga over his business suit, but he later loosened up and took off the business suit. We had the video of *Animal House* playing and also the sound track from the movie. We had limbo contests, a guitarist, and a cake shaped like an old Buick.

I invited a lot of people so that the room would be crowded, which always helps a party. We took old sheets and decorated them like a fraternity house. My clients still talk about it and want to be sure they get invited to the next one. We always have a point of reference when we see each other.

My '50s party was a pure dance party. The D.J., "Big Papa," spun the most danceable records behind a fiberglass rendering of an old Mustang. Everyone dressed up in '50s garb—old madras shirts, plaid shorts, poodle skirts, tight jeans, and cigarettes rolled up in the sleeves of white tee shirts. We did "ladies' choice" so that everyone had an opportunity to rock and roll plus lots of line dancing, which doesn't require a partner.

I made sure that my clients had the best time that they could have and were treated like royalty. I made certain they were introduced to everyone, were personally taken to the front of the food line, and had all their favorite records spun. I did it because I wanted them to see how much I cared for and valued them not just as clients but as people.

Parties don't have to cost a lot. But when you don't spend a lot of money, you have to spend a lot more time and imagination. Food does not have to be elaborate, it just has to be abundant. It is much more appealing to have two or three large plates and bowls that are overflowing than a lot of small items that require both a great deal of work and more money.

A PARTY FOR ALL THE RIGHT REASONS

Parties happen for all kinds of reasons. One of my advertising clients had spent four months working on obtaining a large, national fast-food chain. Everyone in the entire firm was involved, and the excitement of having this food company as a client electrified the entire office. Many personal and family commitments were put aside, and all energies were focused on this project.

But my client didn't get the contract. It went to another advertising agency.

The office was devastated. They were hurt, angry, and indignant. No one was bouncing back. Other projects were languishing. The president called everyone together and gave them a pep talk, but to no avail. Too much energy had been used up and too much creativity expended without result.

The president decided that drastic measures must be taken to turn his office around and get productivity back. He invited his entire office, which he had never done before, to his home. He had a "Competitor's Party," which meant that everyone feasted on fast food from the competing chains of their once-potential client. The decorations were a satirical take-off on the former client's restaurant. He wrote and produced a skit that good naturedly but pointedly helped define the feelings of frustration that everyone in his office was experiencing.

The party was a great success. What he accomplished could never have been done at a restaurant, hotel, or through prolonged staff meetings. The sentence had been handed down to the firm and the only thing to do was get everyone back on track, feeling positive and empowered again. The party at his home did it.

POINTERS FOR SUCCESSFUL
BUSINESS ENTERTAINING AT HOME

1. Invite your guests to help you prepare or serve the food. People enjoy best what they are involved in. That is why it is often most fun to start with a casual dinner the first time and then work up to something more formal. Casual affairs invite participation. Generally, formal dinners don't allow much except maybe the carving of the meat or the uncorking and pouring of the wine.

2. Break the ice, but don't accomplish that by pushing liquor. Instead, do your homework on each invited guest so that you can have an engaging discussion with everyone plus give guests conversational information about each other.

3. Do at least one original thing. It can be a stuffed dummy sitting on your front porch dressed up in a business suit with a sign that says "Welcome Mr. Higgins," if your boss or client has a sense of humor. Or it can be one beautiful flower on every person's plate.

4. Don't spend more than you can afford. Don't try to impress business associates with lavish spending. The best parties are those that bring people together emotionally, and that has more to do with

chemistry and lively conversation than expensive wine and imported caviar.

5. Don't invite friends the first time you invite your boss to dinner. You don't want to look insecure. Also, you want to be free to focus on your boss, not your friends.

If you invite your boss to a larger party, make sure that all your friends know beforehand who he or she is so that no one sticks their foot in their mouth.

6. Don't try French cuisine or any other complicated cooking unless you are very proficient at it. Aim for something that you are very proficient at, even if it means grilled hamburgers, baked beans, and chips with dip.

7. Rent or borrow what you don't own. Business dining at home is to build business, not bankrupt you.

8. Start small and work up. Pizza can lead to primavera, and that can lead to seafood fettucine with lobster sauce. Just don't start with the lobster first.

CHAPTER FIFTEEN

BUSINESS TRAVEL

You are at the end of a four-city business trip and heading home on Friday, anxious to go rafting and camping with your friends. Your flight is delayed twice, first by weather, now by a mechanical "difficulty." After patiently sitting in your seat for forty-five minutes on the ground, you have just been informed that you must change planes.

You collect your papers, stuff them into your briefcase, and tiredly make your way, along with the rest of the passengers, to the designated gate. As you elbow your way aboard the new plane, it is clear that your originally assigned bulkhead seat has been taken. It is now occupied by a weary-looking woman holding a baby with a five-year-old girl seated beside her. You don't have the heart to ask them to move.

You ask the harried flight attendant for help and she points to the last seat in coach. You are now wedged between a teenager with her Sony Walkman and a chatty older man who is delighted that you haven't tuned him out with ear phones so that you two can become "really good friends."

Is traveling worth the trouble? Can we maintain a powerful professional presence on the road? Of course!

THE TRAVEL ADVANTAGE

As effective as the telephone is, it will never replace the reassurance of a personal meeting between a buyer and a salesperson; a patient and a doctor; a stockbroker and a client. Lyndon Johnson, even in ill-health, insisted on a face-to-face meeting with the Vietnamese in Hawaii. Signed documents, phone calls, and assurances by top-level officials aren't as conclusive as the power of a personal meeting.

Many people get their best ideas while traveling. Their energy flows, and their creative juices get a jolt from new faces and new places. Traveling can be energizing and can clear out the cobwebs.

Three presidents of companies with whom I work closely have confided that they often attend out-of-town trade shows or conventions just so that they can have a day to break the routine of their office work and think more creatively. Traveling rejuvenates their imagination and gives them a fresh perspective.

Often, associates will have almost unlimited access to their boss during road trips. This kind of uninterrupted time can be invaluable. Gripes can be aired and thoroughly discussed, industry gossip and ideas can be exchanged, and helpful information can be passed on in an environment with much less time constraint than on the telephone or at a sales meeting.

Business relationships can be cemented by travel because the relationship becomes multi-dimensional and often more personal. Your boss's passion for estate sales and antiques may never have surfaced at the office but will become an important link to a closer relationship with you when it is discussed in length over an unhurried, out-of-town dinner. And if you enjoy traveling with your boss, tell him or her; it is a genuine compliment. If you don't enjoy the company, then schedule your trip either prior to or after their flight and plan only one dinner together.

GETTING THERE AND DOING THE JOB

Business travel, despite its benefits, can be long on stress. It can erode the composure and presence that are much easier to maintain on our own home turf. Whatever method you use to travel, the effort of getting there is sometimes more work than the actual labor of transacting business.

One of my clients who recently started traveling as a consulting engineer said that she was exhausted by the time she finally arrived in her designated city and just wanted to head to the hotel and sleep. She felt she had done her job for that day just by traveling six hours. "Travel is work enough. I dragged my luggage from the plane to the metro to the cab. I can't imagine that I will ever have the stamina to see clients, too!"

It does take stamina, as well as grace and a sense of humor, to be a productive business traveler. You may love traveling, hate it, or simply tolerate it, but until we have the technology to "Beam us up, Scotty," face-to-face encounters requiring travel will continue to be one of the bases for doing business.

One problem is that business people often overschedule their travel so that by the time they arrive at the important meeting, they have lost a great deal of their effectiveness due to being stressed out. Overeating and overdrinking will wear out even the strongest person. Running on all eight cylinders on the road means that you will be burned out and broken down when you get back to the home office. If a meeting is important, allow an extra night to rest.

Try changing the pace and relaxing in unusual ways. For instance, instead of eating a huge, fattening meal that probably would get in the way of a good night's sleep, opt for a relaxing massage instead. They cost about the same. Most large hotels have health clubs that offer massage.

If you have the time, see a play. Most people don't think about the theater unless they are in New York City. There are usually fine performances in all cities, and often great single tickets are available thirty minutes before the performance. Opera, classical concerts, and rock concerts can also be a real treat. Losing yourself in a live performance is a wonderful way to de-stress and rejuvenate. If you and your significant other differ in your taste of movies, this is the time to see what you like.

It can be fun to get a manicure or pedicure, too. Just don't try a haircut or hair color out of town, unless you have a strong personal recommendation from someone you really trust. Don't let the intrigue of new surroundings cloud your good judgment.

THE GRACEFUL TRAVELER

Those who possess presence have mastered the art of being a graceful traveler; they seldom complain about the unavoidable difficulties and delays of travel. They also know when it's possible to change circumstances by complaining successfully and when to remain quiet and make the best of things. They have a sense of priority, of knowing what is really important, and that gives them added power over their circumstances.

It's obvious that no airline, bus service, or car rental company wants to delay passengers. This is expensive both in terms of money and loss of customer loyalty. So, although you have a right to get straight answers, yelling at the employees usually doesn't accomplish anything.

Handling delays with grace is part of having professional presence. In the airport you can always retreat to an airline club and make phone calls, read a report, or watch television. In other locations, you can buy some ice cream, get a paperback novel, or catch up on your business reading.

KEEPING COMFORTABLE ALOFT

Although trains have certainly made a comeback for pleasure travel and buses are favored by John Madden and Cher, the majority of business travelers get to where they need to go by car or plane. Let's take a look at some airline issues first.

The more relaxed you are in your travels, the more impressive you will be when you arrive. Long airline flights require that you exercise. Walk to the restroom and just stand there near the door. You could even read a magazine, or flip through a report, while stretching. If someone starts to queue up behind you, just wave them past and continue your reading and leg stretching.

Do isometric exercises in your seat. Start with your toes, curling and uncurling them, and work up. Move to the balls of your foot and back on the heel. Press palms together and release. Roll your shoulders forward and backward. Circle your head. Getting your circulation and muscles moving will make the trip more tolerable, and you will experience less jet lag at the other end.

Mental comfort is also important. If a nearby passenger is doing something that is annoying, you can politely handle the issue yourself. For instance, if I end up with a large person dozing off and drooling on my shoulder during the flight from Atlanta to Seattle, a gentle but firm repositioning saves on dry-cleaning bills.

If the issue is one that you prefer not to address directly, inform the flight attendant. Although that option may feel like squealing to the teacher in class, it is usually better quietly to address any major grievance to a flight attendant. For instance, if a passenger has an offensive odor, you probably aren't the only one complaining. If someone is loud and drunk, everyone will be affected. Even for a relatively minor issue, such as being too hot or too cold, inform the attendant.

If you inadvertently disturb or offend someone, then handle the incident as diplomatically as possible. And always apologize. A sincere "I am so sorry" goes a long way.

I was once seated next to a businessman who obviously liked to talk and flirt, but he seemed pretty harmless, so I listened to him for a while. As he spoke, he was nervously flicking the end of his swizzle stick with his thumb. Suddenly it flew out of his hand, grazed my eye, popped out my contact lens, and landed on the tray table in the next aisle. He was mortified as I crawled around looking for my lens.

But he profusely apologized, gave me his card, and promised to buy ten copies of my book for his staff. His sincerity canceled out his transgression.

ARM WRESTLING AND OTHER AIRLINE GAMES

Armrest etiquette, as simple as it seems, can generate bad feelings on an airplane. If you end up in the center seat and the other two passengers have claimed both armrests, you will be left like a sardine in the middle feeling resentful and ready to strangle your travel agent.

The proper etiquette is that the middle person, being more squeezed and inconvenienced, gets two armrests. The other two passengers each get one armrest because one has the window for a sense of space, and the other can go the restroom and stretch as many times as needed.

Patience and goodwill can minimize difficulties. I walked into a packed airplane recently and sat down across the aisle from a mother with a baby. This little pink-faced cherub was wailing and her mother was frantic, trying to bounce her, pat her, feed her, and juggle toys in front of her. Along came a big bad business man who was assigned to the seat right next to the duo. He scowled, glared at the hapless mother, and immediately started making a fuss to the flight attendant. The poor mother just wilted.

This scene is repeated hundreds of times each day, although the business person could just as well be a silk-suited woman, and the parent, a harried father. It's not fair to blame a parent for having a child that needs to be on your flight. Traveling families are a fact of life.

I think, however, that since smoking and non-smoking sections have been virtually eliminated, the airlines should consider a baby and non-baby section. Everyone would be happier. Business people could swap business cards while parents could swap baby stories. Until things change, what should a savvy business person do in this situation?

The appropriate thing is to sit down, smiling benignly at the parent and child. After the plane takes off, murmur your apologies about having to do a report and look for another seat. Or quietly ask the flight attendant if someone with a child would want to trade. Never harangue the parent, frown at the child, or give the cold shoulder. In my business travels I have been accidently kicked, hit by flying Play-Doh, thrown up on, wet on, and wailed at by many an unhappy child, and I'm still here to talk about it. No parent wants an unhappy camper on a crowded airplane, but infants and very young children simply can't be switched on and off for the comfort of others.

EATING AND DRINKING IN FLIGHT

I love to bring popcorn on the plane, but I try to resist the urge. Having someone crunch in your ear certainly isn't pleasant. If you are ravenous, try to eat before you get on the plane. If you do bring food on, select only neatly eaten food—no ice-cream bars with the chocolate dripping off the sides—and try to eat it when other meals are being served. Your snack shouldn't be overly messy or too fragrant. A Limburger cheese and onion sandwich, for example, would probably find you sitting alone.

The best advice in terms of liquor is not to drink at all. But if you do, limit your drinks to one on short flights and two on longer ones. If you travel frequently between the same cities, chances are you may run into clients, coworkers, or the competition. There is no point in ruining your presence by appearing a little too gassed up.

If you don't drink, you will arrive much more refreshed and suffer less from jet lag. But if the liquor is free, which it always is in first class, and often is if the plane takes off late, then the temptation is usually too great. Even drinks in coach are very reasonable and can take the edge off a long trip. Just remember that one drink on the ground is the equivalent of two in the air, and if you love to talk, you will definitely become more loquacious with your seatmates.

PACKING SMART

1. Pack as light as possible. On overnight trips, organize your garments so you can bring your luggage on the plane. With either long or short trips, anticipate your activities. Decide what garments will be required and make a list. Sometimes it is as easy as taking three strong business outfits and one fuzzball-covered sweatsuit with no requirements for anything else. Women should pick one primary color, like black, so that a minimum of accessories will be needed. For a week-long trip, pack two suits and wear the third one. For fewer wrinkles during the trip, a woman can turn her skirt around and sit on the front of it. Then when she arrives, she can readjust her skirt with virtually no wrinkles in the front and her jacket hiding the ones in the back.

For long trips, wear comfortable clothes and pack all three outfits. Darker garments are safer because dirt, spots, and stains are much less apparent on a navy suit than on a khaki one.

2. Don't pack a bathrobe. Many hotels provide them. If not, you can always answer the door with your coat on.

3. If you exercise, bring the minimum amount of exercise gear. Leotards or running shorts are easy to pack. Swimming is great because it requires so little in the way of apparatus, but be sure to bring plastic bags in case you have to pack a wet suit. Insert athletic shoes into old woolen socks or wrap in plastic dry-cleaning bags to make sure they don't get anything else dirty.

4. Pack one pair of dark, comfortable business shoes and wear a second pair of business shoes. They can be polished at the airport or hotel. Both men and women should go for comfort. Never bring a new pair of shoes on a trip.

5. Don't bother bringing a travel iron or a hair dryer. Even economy hotels will supply them if you call ahead. But do include a small, collapsible umbrella.

6. Select suits and blouses that need a minimum of pressing on arrival, or better yet, don't need to be pressed at all. Expensive silk or wool doesn't wrinkle much. Inexpensive silk or wool wrinkles greatly. Purchase a tie case to keep ties smooth and clean.

To further minimize wrinkling, try these ideas:

a. Wrap easily wrinkled items in tissue paper or plastic dry-cleaning bags.

b. Keep the plastic dry-cleaning bags intact on suits and then pack everything into a garment bag.

c. Bring a can of "wrinkle-free" spray.

d. Ask for a cardboard garment box at airport check-in for soft-sided luggage or garment bags. Most are sturdy so they can be recycled for future trips.

7. If you travel a great deal, have duplicate cosmetic items. Keep

your travel shampoo, shaver, shaving cream, mascara, blush, eye shadow, and anything else you need in a separate cosmetic bag or travel kit that never gets used at home. It makes it a breeze to pack because everything is prepacked.

(8) For peace of mind, take along expensive jewelry only if it can be worn all the time. Watches, rings, and bracelets that work with your travel wardrobe are fine. Earrings, necklaces, and cuff links can be easily lost or stolen. Hotel rooms are not safe places to store valuables. Put jewelry in your carry-on baggage, not in checked luggage.

(9) Purchase luggage that won't embarrass you when you lift it off the conveyer belt or bring it into a hotel. It's just as important as your briefcase or handbag.

(10) Be sure to put identification tags on everything. A business address is safer than a home one. Don't waste time at the airport filling them out. Have them already attached. Even carry-on bags should have a luggage tag. If you have ever left a briefcase at a pay phone, you will understand the wisdom of identifying everything.

TIPS ON TIPPING

Nothing is more embarrassing than having only a $50 bill when you need a $2 tip. Keep a roll of at least ten $1 bills in a convenient pocket for quick, discreet tipping.

In a hotel, tip a dollar per bag up to two bags. Then it is usually about fifty cents per bag unless the bellperson has provided unusual service like getting ice, spending ten minutes telling you about the best restaurants in town, or arranging for an iron and ironing board to be brought up immediately.

You can save on tipping at the airport if you bring your own bags inside. Otherwise, at curbside the appropriate tip is $1 for the first bag and fifty cents for each additional bag. If you are late for your flight, wave a $5 bill for more immediate service and tell the skycap to expedite your luggage.

Cab drivers generally receive between 10 and 15% of the fare depending on their politeness, how carefully they drove, and the cleanliness of their cabs. If your cab ride lacks these amenities, just pay the fare.

A CLEAN CAR IS A BLISSFUL CAR

If driving is your preference and you will be using your vehicle to transport others, make sure your car stays both clean and organized. Not many people would bring their customers or clients into a home with trash on the floor, with visibly smudged windows, or candy-bar wrappers stuffed between the seats of the couch. But they don't seem to give a second thought to driving customers around in a grubby car.

Research has indicated that people feel depressed when they drive a dirty car. It is hard to perform professionally when the steering wheel is greasy from french fries, or mud from a camping trip is still on the carpet, or you have to sift through piles of old newspapers on the floor to find your account book.

If you drive for business, you will be rewarded for having a clean car. A spotless automobile makes a great first impression when you are taking clients out to dine or just picking them up at the airport. I can't count the number of times that someone has greeted me at the airport, and almost before saying hello, has blurted out, "My car is a real mess and I never got around to cleaning it. Sorry!"

But even if you don't carry others in your car, the personal benefit of having a clean car is worth the trouble it takes to clean it. You feel organized, clean, and efficient. You can also feel assured that there's no risk of sitting on a leftover tuna fish sandwich and ruining your suit.

ROMANCE ON THE ROAD

Never invite a client or customer back to your hotel room. It simply isn't worth the risk of being misunderstood. If they need to get something that is in your room, ask them to wait in the lobby or have the bellman deliver it to their room.

When I was traveling extensively for a cosmetics company, one of my saleswomen innocently went back to a salesman's room to get some samples for a training session held the next morning. As he was digging around in his sample case, his phone rang and without thinking, he asked her to grab it. It was his wife who wasn't too thrilled that a woman was answering his phone at 10:00 at night. She icily asked for her husband.

It was embarrassing for my saleswoman, humiliating for the sales-man, and infuriating for the spouse. Also, why risk the implication of a coworker seeing you leave someone else's room at a late hour if other arrangements can be made?

You also never really know when something can come back to haunt you. I was recently at a meeting where twelve of us had arrived by plane from different parts of the country. Unknowingly, two of the attendees had sat beside each other on a flight. Brian had made pretty clear sexual advances toward Michelle after ten minutes of conversation. She quickly refused them and they didn't speak much during the rest of the flight. He was mortified when he saw Michelle entering the same session he was attending the next morning. Affairs of the heart on the road are not only dangerous but may also be an assault on a business reputation. They may provide temporary distraction, but they can end up creating a great deal more stress.

MORE POINTERS FROM SEASONED TRAVELERS

If you have access to a helicopter, private jet, and chauffeur-driven limousine, plus an entourage of private minions to plan your itinerary, then maximum travel efficiency would be assured. Unfortunately, this is not the reality for most of·us who must travel.

Clients cancel out, appointments get changed, and colleagues fail to show up at the airport. Unexpected things do happen. Illness, family problems, and other urgent business cannot be planned. Therefore, confirm and reconfirm appointments and flight times to maximize your time on the road. Never set up an appointment and assume it stands. Follow up with a fax or letter, and at least one phone call, which should be in the afternoon prior to your travel day.

Confirming plans accomplishes two things. One, the date and place are clearly established. Two, you position your time as limited and your presence as valuable. With follow-up, 99% of scheduled meetings will happen as planned.

Unless you are in a business that has a lot of emergencies, don't check back with your office more than once a day. It eats up a lot of time, and most situations can wait until you are less pressured. Instruct both your office staff and family not to discuss issues with you that you can't do anything about. If the copy machine broke down and it will take another forty-eight hours to fix, have your office take care of it. If the next-door neighbor has put up a huge satellite dish in the front yard, what can you do about it from two thousand miles away?

Along the same line, don't have major arguments over the phone with people in the office. When feeling out of control because of distance, the situation is usually exacerbated. Do damage control and then wait until you are back at the office to really effect a solution.

TEN SPECIFIC IDEAS FOR BUSINESS TRAVEL

1. Bring business stationery and envelopes in a large envelope. Quick agreements can be executed and important letters sent immediately.

2. Travel with at least one granola bar, or emergency snack.

3. Make sure at least two people from your office, plus your family, have your hotel phone number.

4. Keep an emergency first-aid kit in your briefcase. Sixty-two percent of all business travelers suffered from some physical ailment

in the past year. It is hard to have power and professional presence when you are suffering from a upset stomach, headache, indigestion, a cold, or a cough.

(5.) Never dress shabbily for a flight. You never know who you will meet on the plane.

(6.) You are responsible for the total area that you create with your belongings. Watch how you swing that hanging bag or bulky shoulder luggage as you walk down the aisle. Clipping the head of a fellow passenger, though unintentional, is rude.

(7.) In most cases, be sure your last appointment knows your departure schedule. However, if you are in serious negotiations, don't give away your departure time.

(8.) Bring along a framed picture of your favorite person, dog, or cat for your hotel room. It will bring warmth and connection to you after a long day.

(9.) Order flowers, fruit, or a plate of homemade cookies through the hotel to welcome an out-of-town customer. This kind of thoughtfulness makes a wonderful impression. And if you feel entitled to it, order the same for yourself if you have had a weary flight.

(10.) Bring one stretched out, worn-out, and totally comfortable tee shirt and pants for relaxing. This is the perfect outfit to wear at the end of a long day of business meetings when you flop on your bed, switch on an in-room movie, and order room service.

Part VI

◆

COMMAND PERFORMANCES

CHAPTER SIXTEEN

CORPORATE PARTIES AND SALES MEETINGS

Command performances in the business world include the office party, client cocktail parties, the company picnic, social invitations from your boss, the hospitality suite at the sales meeting, the Christmas party, the "Spring Prom" (as one of my clients refers to their formal dinner dance), and any organized sports event, cultural event, honorary dinner, or invitation to The Club.

The dichotomy that corporate events present is that they are specifically planned to break down barriers and loosen up behavior. Yet everyone there is being scrutinized to see how well they behave.

A major corporate function is the perfect time to ruin your career in one fell swoop. Everyone who has control over your career and your advancement will be in attendance. That is the main reason most employees have a strong urge to stay home.

Let me borrow a technique that a late night television host uses in introducing important topics—The Top Ten List. This list, however, has to do with the top ten major mistakes that an unsuspecting employee can make at a corporate function. All we need to do is go to one business affair to see nearly every one of these at work.

(1) Not showing up. The first rule of business functions is that you can't ignore them. You must show up. You may leave early, if you have to, but you need to make your entrance no later than thirty minutes after the expressed time on the invitation.

Aside from showing up, you have a mandate to attend the company-sponsored hospitality suite for at least an hour. You also have the responsibility to partake in games, dancing, roasting of the president, or whatever else the social committee has thought up.

You may not stay glued to your buddies all night. The whole reason for the event is to mix and mingle with new colleagues and higher-ups with whom you generally have limited contact. But the irony is that the empty seat at dinner is always next to the president. Most people's comfort zone is with peers, not superiors.

(2) Ignoring the boss, the president, or the chairman because you are afraid of making a faux pas. Employees who ignore their boss at corporate function are rarely rewarded, promoted, or otherwise recognized. It is like being invited to a birthday party and ignoring the birthday boy or girl; don't expect an invitation for next year. But the more socially inept your boss is, the more gratitude will be felt if you come to the rescue on social occasions.

So why not stretch a little, show some power and presence, and possibly further your career? At minimum, greet the most senior people at a corporate affair and spend three or four minutes talking with each one. Appropriate topics of conversation are the generosity of the company for footing the bill, the festive food and ambiance, light topics of business, and any known hobbies of the host or hostess.

One thing we have all found out about small talk—the more we do it, the easier it gets. The fact is most senior people feel just as awkward and uncomfortable as you and probably more so because they are expected to be smooth and charming.

(3) Believing that "business casual" means jeans and a tee shirt. Dressing for the occasion is important to your sense of power and self-confidence. If the affair is formal, be certain that you show up in a tuxedo, not a suit. If you attend two or more social events annually that require a tuxedo, plan to purchase one. It will fit better and it is always available.

As a female employee or a male employee bringing a date, find out whether the skirt length will be short or long. Black is always a safe color and velvet, silk, satin, and sequins are wonderful for evening events. Just don't wear anything too sexy, too tight, or too revealing.

If you can't afford to buy something lovely, look in the yellow pages for stores that rent formal wear. Nearly all of them rent dresses and gowns, too.

On the other end of the spectrum is "business casual," one of the most misunderstood and misinterpreted terms in business vernacular. It isn't what you would wear to hang around the house watching football or horsing around with the kids on Sunday afternoon. It doesn't include cutoffs, tee shirts, tank tops, blue jeans, shorts, warm-up suits, or thongs.

Business casual means well-coordinated outfits. Ralph Lauren or a good imitation is a very upscale look for men. An all-cotton, well-pressed, blue striped shirt with khaki pants, argyle socks, and deck shoes plus a cotton sweater for cooler evenings is very appropriate. Shorts are not appropriate for daytime meetings, but can certainly work for a luau on the beach.

For women, well-tailored trousers with coordinating blouses or sweaters define business casual. Longer, fuller skirts with turtleneck tops look polished and professional for daytime sessions. Earrings, scarfs, and shoes should be as well coordinated as with any business suit. Summer dresses are a better choice than shorts for events that will take you outside.

④ Gossiping about your boss. When you are away from home, in a small group in a smokey bar, it seems the perfect time to let down your guard and express how you really feel about the person you work for. No one has a perfect boss. They don't exist. But why point out their frailties? When everyone else is spilling the beans on the boss, it is almost irresistible not to add your two cents about how she regularly loses her temper or how he has a drinking problem.

Sometimes you will be asked to confirm a rumor about your boss such as, "I hear he got passed over for the vice presidency because he's gay." Loyalty is always rewarded. So is having the presence not to give credence to any rumor, true or not, about your boss.

It is interesting that topics of conversation that would never be broached in the office become lively talk at a sales meeting. Illustrating a powerful presence may simply mean that you stretch, yawn, and excuse yourself. It would be rare that any juicy morsel that you offer *wouldn't* get back to the boss.

⑤ Overeating and overdrinking. When you significantly overeat or overdrink at a company function, it appears rather low class, as if you rarely get out. One of my seminar attendees sheepishly told me that he got the nickname of "Goober" because he ate so ravenously and even took doggie bags with him at company events.

Early in her career, one of my associates embarrassed herself by eating so much that when she stood up, her belt popped open and fell off in a loud clatter. As she bent over to pick it up she burped loudly. At that point, she wanted to stay bent over and crawl under the table.

If you love to eat and have a huge appetite, enjoy a large snack before going to an event (Scarlett O'Hara did it) where you will be dining with business colleagues and clients. Or eat after the event is over. And think twice about bringing anything home.

6. Cheating on the golf or tennis courts. It is very hard to have presence when you are playing a sport with a cheater. During the later months of my pregnancy, I spoke at a national sales meeting and was asked to join the group for free time in the afternoon. I decided to play chess with one of the attendees.

Although I am not an especially accomplished chess player, I had her in "check" because she made a poor move. I proceeded to grab her piece when she said loudly and with authority, "I would like to evoke the five-second rule." I looked at her as though she was crazy. "The what?" I said.

"Why, the five-second rule, which means that I have five seconds to change my mind and move my piece to another place on the board." Being eight months pregnant, I decided I probably had more important considerations than risking my health by jumping up and flinging the chess board across the room, though at the time I seriously considered doing it.

It is extremely difficult to be fully aware of cheating and not be able to do much about it. One of my clients always receives a request to play tennis with the president's wife at the company picnic. If the boss's wife is losing, she frequently calls her opponent's balls "out" when they are not even a close call. My client decided that it wasn't worth debating over, but she harbors resentment about playing with her.

Professional presence prescribes that you use meaningful looks, a raised eyebrow or two, or a slight rolling of the eyes when your boss shaves points off the "ole" golf game. Meaningful body talk is almost as gratifying as jumping up and down and shouting, "Why you cheater!! You know it took you twelve strokes to get the ball in." Almost as gratifying, but not quite. Still, you walk away with your dignity intact, your honesty unflawed, and your job secure. Yet you have also been given an important clue: The way someone plays on the sports field is often how they play in the boardroom.

Good sportsmanship is allegorical to business. In fact, chess was created by war-weary leaders so that kings could fight their battles on the chessboard, not the battlefield. The same qualities that are admired in sports are equally admired in business: strategy, persistence, strength, a desire to win, and a sense of fair play.

Good rules for any sport include:

- Being perfectly honest about your ability in the sport.
- Being not only on time but early and ready to play, with the right equipment and the correct attire.
- Never getting angry with the poor performance of your opponent or yourself. Try not to swear.
- Taking your intensity level from your host. If this is just a relaxing game of golf designed to build comradery, don't play as though you are in the finals at The Masters. On the other hand, don't be a goof-off on the tennis court if you are playing with a serious player.

⑦ Making a pass at another company employee. Company picnics, quarterly beer parties, and impromptu office celebrations encourage us to look at each other in a different light. Away from the pale fluorescence of an office cubicle, a coworker can take on a whole new light. Or at least in a smiling, happy atmosphere, the rules seem to get fuzzy.

One of my male clients was flabbergasted when a secretary who had enjoyed one beer too many came up and grabbed his derriere. She looked at him and said, "You know, I have just always wanted to do that." And then she walked away.

One of my single, female clients got roped into playing "spin the new bottle" with the new cola product that her company had just introduced. But the twist was that the two partners couldn't kiss; they had to find another body part to pair up. Most just giggled and shook hands or rubbed shoulders. But the married human resources director gave my client a lingering, full-body embrace. It clearly wasn't innocent. It was an intentional pass.

A public or a private pass can boarder on sexual harassment. Don't encourage one and certainly don't make one. You will lose power, respect, and credibility.

(8.) Losing your cool with a celebrity. Large companies often sponsor parties during industry conventions. These events generally hinge around well-known stars. Nationally recognized personalities like football players, coaches, television news people, or best-selling authors are frequently invited to make a presentation at huge dinner meetings.

It is a wonderful feeling to have people wildly applaud and show enthusiasm. But I watched with a mixture of amusement and embarrassment as two mature company employees clung onto the lead singer of a music group after the performance. They figured that since their company had sponsored the event, they were entitled to some extra attention. I have also seen full-grown men fall off the stage trying to shake hands and slap the back of an NFL coach.

Don't lose your cool around celebrities. Walk up, shake hands, comment on their stellar performance, and then make way for someone else.

(9.) Missing your boss's big moment. Most meetings require the participation of at least a score of in-house executives. Some are adept at public speaking and others fairly faint at the thought.

Stay close and very loyal to your boss before, during, and after the big moment. Plan to go early to bed the night before the scheduled speech. Don't even think about closing down the bar that evening. Be energized, helpful, and completely supportive. Pass out handout material, shepherd people into the room, clap loudly, and generally carry on like Ed McMahon. Your boss will love you for it!

Be ready to step in if necessary. A vice president of a computer company had to pinch-hit at the last minute because its president and CEO was literally getting sick in the men's room ten minutes prior to his address to the industry council. Donald stepped in and eloquently took over. To this day, the president is still grateful to his loyal vice president for saving the evening.

(10.) Believing that you can make a fool of yourself and everyone will forgive and forget. Don't think for a minute that what you do at an off-site meeting will not get back to the office and possibly your home. The problem with walking on the wild side at a business function, is that you can't win. Casting yourself as a fool, flake, or drunk totally misses the raison d'être of being at the affair.

Don't go to the hotel room of someone of the opposite sex, unless a whole group is going. Don't go out bar hopping with the gang, unless you are certain things will stay under control. You will never be faulted for being circumspect, but you could end up in jail if you are party to anything rowdy or illegal.

One of my clients was offered cocaine by her boss at a convention in Las Vegas. At the time she had only been with the company for three months. Although she was shocked, she discreetly declined and found out later that he did that routinely, but it was actually a bogus substitute.

He did it purely to see what kind of reaction he would receive and to gauge the level of integrity of his new hires, although he was severely reprimanded when one of his employees reported him to personnel.

Don't allow peer pressure to engage you in an activity that you know will somehow not enhance your reputation. One of my former colleagues went skinny-dipping with five other colleagues of the opposite sex, and forevermore they were referred to as the "Navy Seals." This, of course, required an explanation every time it was mentioned in front of someone not privy to their escapades.

PARTIES TO DECLINE

There are some invitations that you probably want to immediately decline. One of the no-win company parties is the pool party. Often when an executive from the company has a new pool installed, a party seems in store.

But for a female employee, let's look at the reality. First, if you have a well-exercised body with no additional fat or cellulite anywhere, everyone will stare in adoration or lust. Remarks will be made and you may feel victimized. That group of women comprises about .0005% of the population.

The rest of us who are not centerfolds will be forced to display our half-naked bodies before every man in the office, who previously had only seen the flesh on our face, our hands, and twelve inches of our leg. Either way, it's a no-win situation.

For men who are extremely out of shape with a large stomach and thin legs, there will still be the requisite "once over" by the group. Because of social conditioning, most men probably won't feel as scrutinized as women do, but most out-of-shape men will admit to being uncomfortable.

If you have the option, attend the pool party in a nice summer outfit that will give you a better comfort level in front of your peers. You don't have to get wet to enjoy yourself.

If you are attending a meeting at a resort where beach activities are planned, both men and women should shop for the most flattering bathing suit and wear a cover-up to and from the beach.

Other events to approach with caution are high-stake poker games and individual sports events where you have no proficiency whatsoever.

A GENEROUS GESTURE

One of the nicest compliments that is ever paid to me is when one of my clients or vendors invites me to an important company event. To be included in a "family affair" is a wonderful show of generosity and is quite an honor to the person receiving the invitation.

Looking at it from a company's perspective, why not maximize all the expense, time, effort, and imagination that is required for a major event? You can generate additional goodwill and public relations by inviting an "extended business family." It may be as elaborate a tradition as the annual Christmas party, a friendly event like the company picnic, or a hot event like a live concert, where the company springs for all the tickets plus buses to the coliseum.

Look over your client list and create a slate of your favorite customers. Invite ten or more. There is no doubt that they will be flattered because this is not an invitation that they would regularly receive. Few firms do this. You are singling them out and showing them that they are more than just business contacts. They are valued friends whom you enjoy not only on a professional basis but on a personal one, too.

CHAPTER SEVENTEEN

YOUR SPOUSE OR PARTNER: AN ASSET OR A LIABILITY?

A client in our office building in Atlanta told me that he begged his pregnant wife to accompany him to the annual Christmas party. He felt he just couldn't go to the affair alone. She went, protesting that her dress was ugly and her feet were swollen.

She whined and complained all night to everyone who would listen. The food gave her gas, she couldn't drink, her shoes were too tight, the baby was kicking, and why was the band so noisy?

Another associate of mine told me that she invited her new boyfriend to the company picnic. Because she was assigned to coordinate the games, she had to be there early.

He arrived separately, donned a cowboy hat as he emerged from his pickup truck, and walked toward her wearing a tee shirt that said

"So many women, so little time." He strode across the field and gave her a loud kiss.

In both cases, my clients decided they should have gone it alone. Having a spouse or date that doesn't fit in is much worse than being single at a corporate event. Forcing a fit with your partner and your coworkers and clients is a mistake. You will feel a loss of presence and power.

Today, many married couples actually prefer to go it alone even when they have the option of bringing a spouse or date. It is easier, more acceptable, and potentially more productive to go *sans* partner. You then have your presence fully under your control.

WHEN A SPOUSE REALLY HATES YOUR OFFICE PARTY

In the case of a spouse or partner who resists exposure to corporate events, even if you dress them up, coach them on what to do and when to do it, the simple fact is, if they don't know the rules of your business world, you will probably end up with three things:

1. An angry and embarrassed partner.
2. Business associates who have seen right through your failed coaching job.
3. An angry you, because it seems that it shouldn't be that difficult to maintain a certain presence for three hours.

If you have a relationship with someone who really dislikes your business and your colleagues, your presence will not be enhanced by dragging them to a company-sponsored event. If they are outwardly hostile or just clam up, vow to keep your personal and professional lives totally separate. Thousands of business people do so and they thrive.

Allowing your spouse to have defined differences without apology to your staff or clients shows a great deal of confidence on your part. One of my female clients just shrugs when she is asked why she never brings her spouse along to company-sponsored events. "I care about him so much that I don't want to force-fit him into my world."

If your attempts at "Pygmalion" didn't work out, accept it and just don't try it again.

INAPPROPRIATE COMMENTS

I have seen spouses do the strangest things at business affairs. One spouse walked up to the president's wife and said, "I am sure I know your name, but I just can't remember it. What is it again?" The president's wife repeated her name graciously but was quite stunned.

I overheard one husband at the company picnic actively lobbying his wife's boss for a raise. "Laurie isn't very assertive about asking for a raise, but you know and I know that she deserves one."

Spouses and partners, however, are not mechanical robots that can be programmed to say the right thing to the right person at the right time. But it is in everyone's interest to do some briefing about the people at the event, giving a rundown of all the names and relationships of the top officers and the topics of conversation to avoid.

At a patio party that my husband and I hosted, I was talking to one of the spouses who said loudly, "I'm glad they fired Fred. He was driving the whole office crazy and my wife complained every night about him." The problem was that Fred had not been fired. In fact, he was standing about four feet away!

Pillow talk is a wonderful release. Venting anger and frustration to a loved one is healthy. But those discussions should stay in the bedroom, and a spouse should know the difference between the irrational rantings of a stressed-out partner and what are legitimate, rational facts.

At a gathering of three people—myself and two clients—a spouse joined our group, laughing and joking with us. Then she turned to her husband's boss and said, "You know, Tom swears at you in the shower every morning, and I mean every morning!" Even though this was meant to be funny and outrageous, Tom's boss did not forget the remark.

BLINDED BY THE LIGHT OF LOVE

We are often blinded by our affections for a spouse or partner. A bright, well-positioned saleswoman brought her boyfriend of six months to a dinner party that I was giving. He was uncomfortable, so he drank too much and then sat down at my piano. After a few notes he proclaimed loudly to the group, "This is a fine piece of furniture, but as a piano it stinks."

On Monday, she called me to thank me for a lovely time and to ask, "What did you think of Kirk? Isn't he wonderful!" If she could have seen my face, she would have known my answer. Her affection for

him did not allow her to see him as an immature individual who
didn't have the experience or background truly to be a business asset
to this competent and charming woman.

Because she didn't work for me, it was not my place to put my arm
around her and tell her what I really thought. But I never saw him
again with her at business affairs, so someone obviously gave her the
word.

TESTING THE WATERS

A good way to see if your spouse or partner is being well received is
by the tone of voice and the facial expressions of your business
associates when they ask about your partner. If they ask in a perfunc-
tory manner and then look bored with your answer as they change the
subject, they are either neutral or negative.

But if they bring up some clever thing your partner said or if they
ask about a special project that was mentioned at dinner, you can
probably assume that you can continue to include your partner.

THE RIGHT OCCASIONS

The climate changes when a spouse is aboard. Even if the spouse is
charming and very flexible, the other business associates will feel
uncomfortable about excluding them when straight business is being

discussed. Often, pure business matters are sidestepped because of the confidentiality factor.

The only time to bring a partner to a business event is if everyone else will be doing the same thing. If you are the only one to bring your wife or husband to a client dinner, you will put a huge strain on the whole affair.

The trend today is not to include spouses at sales meetings, dinner meetings, and corporate retreats. Most employees of the company are actually relieved because they don't have the pressure of making sure their spouse is happy, introduced, and involved. And companies save a great deal of money.

Also, with so many two-income families, spouses are often wining and dining on their own. One client told me that she and her husband schedule client dinners on the same night so that they can do business independently and have the rest of the evenings in the week to be together.

WHEN YOUR SPOUSE CAN HELP YOU

I have a dear friend whose husband is European. When she has dinner meetings with new clients from Germany, Switzerland, France, or Italy, she brings Walter along. There is an instant rapport and an immediate bond. The clients have a lot in common with Walter and a sense of shared viewpoint. Her global business always progresses better when she brings her husband.

Another colleague told me that she brings her artist husband to industry functions to ask the questions that she wouldn't dare ask.

He can ask the most confidential business questions and not even wince because he is not in the business world.

She is always amazed what he finds out for her by the end of the night. At one convention, through his nonchalant, casual manner, she found out the gross annual billings of nearly all her competitors!

One of my former female bosses had a terrific husband who hit it off with the president of the company. They played tennis together, jogged together, and went on Outward Bound for a weekend. She did a good job for the company, but she was even more bulletproof because of the relationship between her husband and her boss.

If your partner does fit in, play it to the hilt. If your spouse naturally complements your presence, showcase them, bring them along when appropriate, and value them. Create opportunities for him or her to be with clients and associates. It will reflect well on you. This is a powerful asset that not everyone has.

BEING SINGLE IN A COUPLES' WORLD

With few exceptions, most of us will spend at least a few years single in a married, corporate world. It shouldn't pose the problems that it did in the 1950s when wives and husbands were glued together, and unless there was a "real problem" men and women were married by the time they were twenty-three.

Although some singles feel they are being discriminated against and made to feel like half a person without a partner, most married people don't understand why they feel like that.

One of my single friends is in a business that sponsors a lot of formal affairs. She doesn't like to have a partner because she would rather devote her full time to talking to clients and potential clients. She told me that her method was to show up, act like the hostess, and have a wonderful time. She always leaves after the first big group leaves; otherwise she says she would feel it appears she has nothing better to do or that she is just hanging around waiting to be picked up.

She also spends as much time as possible with the wives, both the ones who work at home and those who work outside the home. She makes certain that she shows avid interest in them whether they are discussing a child's bedtime or municipal bonds.

Most spouses are flattered and delighted that she genuinely enjoys talking with them because they often know few other people. She also makes a point of introducing her new friends to each other once she sees a connection between them.

Her clients are thrilled because their spouses thoroughly enjoy themselves and feel connected to the event. She enjoys it because she often hears insightful, personal information about her clients. And it also serves to dispense any potential concern with wives because my client frequently travels with their husbands. Her manner is so straightforward, direct, and friendly that gender is not an issue.

THE ROMANTIC GETAWAY—
A HORROR STORY FOR A SINGLE

When a company president decides to take the entire company to Jamaica on a romantic getaway, this can prove extremely uncomfortable for the single employees. Moonlight beach parties, riding two to a moped, and dining in fancy restaurants near the sea is hard to do solo. Married couples look at this as a wonderful opportunity for their "second honeymoon." This means that singles feel as if they are really intruding when they hook up with a couple.

It is usually unacceptable to bring an unmarried partner because most corporate cultures make it very clear that they are not welcome, even if they pay their own way.

Is it OK to forego an extended business "couples" trip? If everything looks as though it will be a disaster, and there won't be any other single people, then do a thoughtful analysis. If you decide that your reputation with your boss will stay intact and that four days and nights of singleness will make you feel self-conscious, obvious, and miserable, then decline.

Another option is to devise a plan for modifying the circumstances to work for you. Stay just part of the time and spend the rest in a location of your choosing. Or organize a few group events where everyone is included and bring a number of wonderful books to read and enjoy the break.

FINDING A METHOD THAT WORKS FOR YOU

We can't always be expected to be the round peg in the round hole. Sometimes a plan is necessary if your circumstances are unusual. One of my clients has a boss whom she describes this way: "She is single, doesn't flirt, works hard, and knows how to have a good time. I think that she was able to get over some of the rough spots about being single at corporate events because we all knew she had a boyfriend back home. He never showed up and she rarely discussed him, but the fact that we thought he existed kept the lechers away and generally added to her independent style."

I have another male client who is fairly young and single, and he has learned to create a scenario which allows him to function well at corporate affairs. He asks a married couple if he can drive with them to the event. He likes to have someone with whom to get the juices flowing; to discuss what the event will entail and to walk in with.

He uses his married colleagues as his comfort zone when he starts to feel a little insecure. Also, because they generally know more people, they introduce him. He never dreads going single to events because his foolproof system makes him feel valued, confident, and assured.

DO'S AND DON'TS FOR MIXING SPOUSES WITH COMPANY EVENTS

1. Don't coax an unwilling spouse to an office function. An obviously resentful attitude on the part of your spouse will reflect badly on you, too.

2. Don't be afraid to go to any corporate event without a partner. You will not lose your power or presence if you maintain an attitude of self-confidence coupled with friendliness.

3. Don't invite a new date to a company event if you are single. Wait until you are comfortable with how they will represent themselves to your office. Fair or not, a date's behavior will reflect on you.

4. Do give your spouse background information on the important people who will be attending a company event. Also, cover issues that should not be discussed.

5. Do introduce your spouse to at least two people and make sure there is conversation going before leaving to join another group.

6. Don't expect to stay at your mate's side the entire evening. This is an important time for him or her to mix and mingle.

7. Don't ever criticize your partner in front of the boss or his or her colleagues.

8. Do always laugh at your spouse's or partner's jokes, even if you are the only one laughing.

9. Don't flirt with anyone at the office in front of your spouse. Don't hug any one of the opposite sex, even if it is completely innocent. Don't create suspicion and complicate your homelife.

10. Do always make your partner look smart, capable, and valued in front of others.

Part VII

◆

GIVING BACK

CHAPTER EIGHTEEN

CORPORATE GIFT GIVING

Thoughtful, appropriate gift giving reveals an elegance, a savvy, and a sense of good breeding that are very important to business. Selecting the right gift both for clients and employees requires a deeper look into what delights them, what they would truly admire.

A corporate gift may be a funny card that reflects a shared sense of humor or a beautifully photographed regional calendar. It doesn't have to be a $75-bottle of cognac. If cost containment is an issue, it is far better and shows a great deal more presence to do something small, personal, and tasteful than to decide you can't afford to do something expensive and just skip the idea entirely.

DEFINING YOUR MARKET

Gift giving breaks down into two areas:

(1) Personal selection of individual gifts. A law firm may take the time personally to select gifts for its top twenty-five clients. One

client may receive a book on hunting, while another receives a signed print from a local artist.

2. Purchasing large numbers of the same gift, which, by definition, will not be individually selected. A newspaper may want to send three hundred Cross pens with their logo to their advertisers as a holiday gift. A real estate company may need fifty congratulatory fruit baskets for new homeowners.

These two types of gifts differ, and it is obvious to a customer receiving one which category they came from. But this doesn't mean that receiving a nice Cross pen with a corporate logo is not a treat. It just means that you have to decide which type of giving is the most appropriate and will create the greatest amount of presence and power for you and your company.

GIVING TO THE INDIVIDUAL

The month of December is the most traditional for corporate gifts to individuals. Gift companies are always busiest then. But the surprise and pleasure of receiving an Executive Planner on Labor Day, a book on bed-and-breakfasts inns three months prior to your vacation, or popcorn and two movie tickets on a Friday morning will certainly create a wonderful impact.

When possible, always personalize the gift with the client's initials, a personal inscription, or the author's or artist's signature. Be sure to include a well thought out, sincere note card, and mention any personal connection that the gift has to the receiver.

GIFTS THAT ARE WELCOME

- A nicely matted and framed photograph or featured newspaper article about that person.
- A book that reflects the person's hobby or an avid interest. Beautiful art books, photography, or unusual cookbooks are always a treasure.

  Hardcover is preferable, but soft cover is fine, too. A great deal is added if the book is autographed by the author. Register with local bookstores so that you can be aware of store-sponsored book signings.

  I have had a number of people send me copies of my first book, *The Professional Image*, with a request for a signature. They also included return shipping to make it easy for me.

  If you don't have the time or the opportunity to get the author's autograph, be certain to do your own inscription in the front.
- A brass carriage clock for office or home with an appropriate engraving on the back.
- Lead crystal, silverplate, or porcelain from a fine store like Tiffany's, Saks, or a quality jeweler.
- Leather goods from a fine store like Mark Cross, Vuitton, or Gucci.
- Brass door knocker with family name.
- A nice print or photograph that has been signed and numbered. Real estate agents and others who rely on long-term referrals should attach their business card on the back of the framed print.
- A video of a favorite old movie.

- A beautifully photographed calendar.
- Cooking paraphernalia like a pasta maker, coffee grinder, or juicer with the appropriate food to accompany them.
- Fine champagne, wine, or cognac for an occasion that is congratulatory, but only if you are certain that it is a favorite brand. Be sure to mention that on the enclosure card.
- Two theater tickets to a popular performance along with a limousine to pick them up.
- Two movie tickets and a box of popcorn to a movie that you have recommended to a customer.
- Golf sweater or golf balls from The Masters or a very special golf course.
- Handcrafted, signed glass paperweight.
- An antique of any sort. The recipient will know it is special but will never know how much it costs.
- Chocolate chip cookies or any homemade goodie. These have special meaning when the treat is made by a single man and presented to a busy mother.

QUANTITY, BUT STILL QUALITY

Just because gifts are ordered in large quantities doesn't mean that the quality and the distinction aren't there. Many family businesses give clients smoked turkeys at Thanksgiving or Christmas, which are a very welcome gift.

One of my clients eagerly anticipates the arrival of two fragrant, fresh fir wreaths from a longtime vendor. For him, it is the harbinger of the holiday season. He doesn't care that the same thing is also sent to two hundred other customers.

If gifts include the company's logo, the quality of the item must be good. In the case of IBM, they not only give quality items, they generally place their logo in a very inconspicuous place. One of my friends still enjoys a lovely crystal fruit bowl, where "IBM" is lightly etched on the bottom and only visible once the fruit is gone. If IBM had been blasted on the side of the bowl, she probably never would have used it.

Nice, quantity gifts:

- Basket of food, which can include either fresh items or boxed ones like gourmet crackers, cheese, and preserves. The best baskets have at least one durable item. Many companies will include an item with a company logo.
- Fresh fruit or hors d'oeuvres on hand-crafted, one-of-a-kind, signed platters bring both an immediate pleasure and a lasting one.

  One company in Washington State keeps an artist busy supplying them with fruit bowls that feature apples, which are then filled with real apples plus a special card, noting how the artist made the hand-crafted bowl. It is a delightful, well thought out corporate gift.
- Regional food that is sent to local clients doesn't have much of an impact. But when smoked salmon is shipped to a customer in Ohio, it is a treat. Other treats might include:
  - Salmon from the Northwest;
  - Peaches, peanuts, and grits from the South;
  - Lobsters and clam chowder from New England;
  - Oranges and grapefruit from Florida or California;

- Steaks from Texas;
- Cheesecake from New York;
- Amish cheese from Pennsylvania or Ohio.
- Good quality chocolate candy with or without a corporate logo. One of my clients sent me a giant chocolate tie in the shape of a fish that I still have today.
- A subscription for a monthly gourmet fruit or coffee delivery to a customer's home.
- Gourmet popcorn in gallon-sized containers.
- A gift certificate to Day Timers.
- A leather portfolio with the recipient's initials on the outside and your corporate logo in an inconspicuous place on the inside.
- A gold pen with recipient's initials engraved on the side and a company logo, if desired.
- A desk set with the client's initials engraved on a small brass plaque.
- A high-quality letter opener with client's initials and small corporate logo, if desired.

CHARITABLE GIFTS

There are other gifts that show presence and a sense of concern for others. Charitable contributions to Meals on Wheels, The Food Bank, The Boy's Ranch, Girl Scouts, The Historical Society, and the YMCA made on behalf of the customer, show a philanthropic concern while honoring your client.

The Professional Image, Inc. has made contributions on behalf of a number of our clients to Atlanta's Table, an organization that collects unserved restaurant food and distributes it to homeless shelters. Once the contributions have been made, we are sent cards to forward to our clients, letting them know that a charitable gift was made by us in honor of them.

The city of Chicago decided that rather than host a $150,000 bash, as a gift from the firms that wrote Chicago's city bonds, the money would be better used by the hungry people of Chicago. Each of the bond houses contributed the same amount of money that they would normally have given to the big society event. It was a gift that demonstrated sensitivity and concern and generated excellent public relations for the firms involved.

ENTERTAINING GIFTS

A very successful lawyer and entrepreneur, Ruth Ackerman, pays a gracious tribute to her field force, who are sales representatives working on commission. She travels to the account executive's city and has dinner with the representative and accompanying spouse. Then the next night she has dinner with whichever potential client the account executive selects.

She wines and dines them at a fine restaurant and pays him or her avid attention. It may either be a customer who has purchased a great deal of advertising, or a business that poses great potential but which hasn't bought a thing. The special evening is Ruth's gift to her salesperson.

Travel agencies often buy blocks of sporting event tickets for their customers. The way they "gift" out the tickets is to let their best customers know they are entitled to four seats per year and that all they need to do is call and request the day. They don't accompany the client to the event but do enclose a personal note along with the tickets that says, "Thanks for using Universal Travel. We hope you enjoy the game."

Symphony, opera, and ballet tickets are wonderful if a company has the right clientele. Otherwise, they just get chucked into the wastepaper basket. Special tickets to the opening of a new play or movie are a wonderful gift, too.

Decide whether an entertaining gift has more presence if you accompany the client, or if it is a more gracious gesture just to send the tickets. It always shows a special touch if you can include something permanent like a wool plaid blanket with football tickets or the compact disc of the opera. But intangible gifts are just as powerful, welcome, and thoughtful as tangible ones.

UNEXPECTED GIFTS

Sometimes the gift that shows the greatest amount of presence is the one not expected. When one of my clients, a company president, took their entire office to San Francisco for a five-day meeting, spouses weren't included. But on the first day of the meeting, each spouse received a large basket of fruit with flowers. The note was personally sent by the president and it said that, although they weren't able to include spouses, the company wanted to show their appreciation for their support.

When I referred one of my clients to another of my clients, they got together and sent me a big Panda bear with a note saying, "A big bear hug and thanks." It was a totally unexpected but clever stroke of creativity.

LOOKING A GIFT HORSE IN THE MOUTH

There are some gifts that are not in good taste or that are simply dated. Wine that is inexpensive or very common is not a good choice. Be very careful you don't give liquor to anyone who is a recovering alcoholic or whose personal convictions or religion forbid it.

Cheap tee shirts or any item made of polyester is better left unpresented. Visors and baseball caps with company logos are generally just thrown in the closet and never worn.

Inexpensive candy, balloons, and ordinary flowers don't have much of an impact.

Anything that is low-grade plastic, useless, or junky, like key chains or bottle cap openers, are a waste of money. So are plastic pens and inexpensive quartz watches with a company logo on the face. Anything that looks like leftover or obsolete inventory is a disaster. It is better to give this away at the company picnic as booby prizes or to find a worthy charity to donate it to.

GLOBAL GIFT GIVING

Although gifts with obvious logos are not always desirable in this country, they are among the most desired of gifts from the United

States in nearly all other countries, with the exception of France. Popular gifts that are highly regarded from American hotels to their Pacific Rim customers are wine decanters and glassware with the hotel logo sand-blasted in the center. Crystal globe paperweights with a company's headquarters pinpointed in color, are very desirable.

Cross pens with logos, especially if they are internationally recognized company logos, are welcome. Status gifts like fine leather goods with logo imprints are good choices. Logo calendars from American firms are very popular in Europe. For an inexpensive gift, Post-it note pads with the company logo will be used and admired.

IS A CARD APPROPRIATE?

Just because someone had a baby doesn't mean you have to send a gift. Just because someone marries doesn't mean you have to find out where they are registered. A gift is never a requirement if you don't attend the occasion.

However, if you attend a boss's, colleague's, or client's invited event, you should bring an appropriate gift. If you are invited but don't attend, then you have the option of a gift or a card. But all important events, whether you are invited or not, require a card if you want to show consideration and presence.

A pregnancy, a retirement, an adoption, and even a divorce may be the right occasion to let a longtime customer know you are thinking about them. It is nearly impossible to overdo sincere cards of congratulation, celebration, and concern for a person's situation.

The death of a loved one is the only time that a purely handwritten note or letter is required.

Keep on hand nice note paper and a cache of various cards, especially hand-crafted cards. These will make it much easier to jot off a quick note.

GIFTS IN THE INNER OFFICE

Some etiquette books will say that it is inappropriate to give your boss a gift. I completely disagree. The gift doesn't have to be expensive, but it is an extremely fine gesture during the holiday season to give your boss a book, a box of favorite chocolates, or an addition to a collection. If it seems more appropriate, you can take up a collection from the staff and purchase a group gift.

I have collected perfume bottles and all types of masks for quite some time and nearly half of them were gifts from my staff. I have everything in my perfume bottle collection from Lalique to fifty-cent curiosities that were purchased at garage sales. My masks have come from fine art galleries and close-out sales. I remember the occasion of each gift and the giver, and I treasure every one of them.

For the boss's birthday, unless the year ends in a big "O," a card signed by the entire office is enough.

In large offices, birthdays can get out of hand. Nearly every day is a birthday for someone. Some large companies with big staffs have one party on the first Friday of the month for everyone with a birthday that month. A cake is purchased, balloons are blown up, candles are blown out, the song is sung, and everyone goes back to work.

An important customer's birthday should always warrant at least a phone call, if not a card, lunch, or small gift.

WRAPPING AND UNWRAPPING

Great care should be given to the wrapping of a business gift. If the wrapping is poorly done or inexpensive looking, it will directly reflect on the present. If a wrapping service is offered where you purchased the gift, pay a little extra for the luxury wrap.

Try to take the time to present the gift in person. This can be done at a client's office or during a business meal.

The gift should be opened immediately and a verbal thank-you, along with well-chosen comments, should be forthcoming. If someone seems confused about whether to open the gift or to wait, graciously suggest that they open it. The exception is with Japanese clients because Japanese manners will not permit them to open a gift in front of the giver.

THE THANK-YOU NOTE

In the South, there is a time-honored tradition that when a gift is received, a thank-you note should be written before the sun sets that day. This is true of both personal and business gifts. If you don't do it then, you are likely to forget the next day, and so it goes until it seems too late to do anything and so you do nothing.

Some political observers say that George Bush won the presidency because of thank-you notes. Over his years in public office, he has written literally thousands of personally penned expressions of his gratitude and appreciation to individuals. That kind of thoughtfulness and consideration is rarely forgotten.

Thank-you notes are important. If you don't send one, that will be remembered. If you do, it may not always be remembered, but you won't have a black mark next to your name in the mind of the giver.

The note should be brief and sincere, and it should certainly mention the gift. Don't refer to the item generically, "Thank you so much for the pen." Instead, try, "Thank you so much for the Mont Blanc fountain pen." State your particular fondness for the item and also discuss how you are going to use it.

A PARTING NOTE

One last word on corporate gifting: Professional presence can never be created solely by giving someone an expensive present. Gift giving can only enhance a business relationship. If even a small gift seems inappropriate, then a simple, sincere, in-person, "Happy Holidays," "Happy Birthday," or "Congratulations on the Baby" is a wonderful, nontangible present. Giving back doesn't need to necessarily be expensive. It just has to be personal.

CONCLUSION

Professional presence, with all the extraordinary opportunities it presents to us, will expand our horizons. It will give us the support, polish, and expertise to venture with assurance into new situations which may previously have appeared intimidating.

Having presence will not guarantee us a smooth ride free of obstacles. We will never hold all the cards in the proverbial card game. There is an old Chinese proverb that states, "The gem cannot be polished without friction, nor man perfected without trials." Incorporating our own, well-developed style of presence will guarantee us that we can confidently handle ourselves well, no matter what the situation.

Professional presence will help you gain and maintain control in business. It will provide the resources to enhance, enrich, and empower your entire career.

—Susan Bixler

INDEX